Becoming God's Last Days Anointed Warrior

Workbook Series

Volume Two

Pray for Strength to Escape

Lessons On

6. Trumpets, Nukes, and a Little Book
7. Warriors for Christ in the Midst of Great Tribulation
8. Spiritual Warfare between The Woman & The Dragon
9. Three Beasts — An Unholy Trinity
10. Mystery Babylon the Capital of Power, Wealth, & Idolatry

A study guide in conjunction with
lectures and video lessons by

DR. DONALD BELL
MAJOR USMC RET.

Becoming God's Last Days Anointed Warrior

Workbook Series Volume Two: *Pray for Strength to Escape*

January 2021

ISBN 978-1-943412-06-8

Published by -
Wilderness Voice Publishing, LLC
Canon City, Colorado USA
www.mcgmin.com

"A voice crying in the wilderness - proclaiming the good news of the coming Kingdom!"

Table of Content

TRUMPETS ------ NUKES
AND
A LITTLE BOOK

(Revelation 8 - 10)

SESSION #6 – WORKBOOK
Intended For
"KINGDOM WARRIORS IN THE ARMY OF GOD"

Unveiling Mysteries in the "Book of Revelation"

Based upon the Book:

GOD'S ANOINTED WARRIORS

By
Dr. Donald Bell
Major USMC, Ret.

(Slides # 2 thru 5)

THE DAWNING OF THE "DAY OF THE LORD"

The opening of the "sixth seal" appears to be the launching of the Day of the Lord;

- This is not a twenty-four-hour day.
- It is a period of time when the Lord will continually manifest Himself through His people in the midst of the greatest devastation in the history of mankind.

But **the day of the Lord** will come like a thief, and then the heavens will pass away with a roar, and the heavenly bodies will be burned up and dissolved, and the earth and the works that are done on it will be exposed. ***2 Peter 3:10***

Another example in Acts 2:19-21

And I will show wonders in the heavens above and signs on the earth below, blood, and fire, and vapor of smoke; the sun shall be turned to darkness and the moon to blood, before the day of the Lord comes, the great and magnificent day. And it shall come to pass that everyone who calls upon the name of the Lord shall be saved. ***Acts 2:19-21***

(Slides # 6 & 7)

THE DAWNING OF THE "DAY OF THE LORD"

The Day of the Lord

Key Points:

- It is a day when the "sixth seal," the seven trumpets" and the "seven bowls of wrath" will successively alter world events and usurp the world's vision of peace and brotherhood without God.
- It is a day when plagues will fall directly on mankind who do not have the "seal of God" on their foreheads.
- It is a day when the "trumpet events" will cause the powers of unbelief and hostility toward God to break into the open in the person of the Antichrist and then, every person's loyalty will become plain.
- It is a day when both forces of righteousness and evil will be so open and clear that every person must declare themselves: either for Christ or for Antichrist.

These plagues being poured out upon the earth are not simply judgments of wrath, but also have a merciful purpose:

- They are designed to turn men, women, and children to God by harsh experiences while the time for decision remains.

Notes:

____

____

____

____

____

____

(Slides # 8 - 9)

THE 6TH SEAL – IS IT NUCLEAR?

Note the repercussions from the 6th seal event:

When he opened the sixth seal, I looked, and behold, there was a great earthquake, and the **sun became black as sackcloth, the full moon became like blood**, and the **stars of the sky fell to the earth** as the fig tree sheds its winter fruit when shaken by a gale. **The sky vanished like a scroll that is being rolled up**, and every mountain and island was removed from its place. ***Revelation 6:12-14***

Key Points:

These characteristics of the 6th seal sound like the after-effects of a nuclear holocaust.

- Smoke from a nuclear blast would certainly cause the **blackening of the sun during the day and the moon to become red** during the night.
- **"Falling stars"** could be nuclear hail also known as "fallout."
- **"Sky vanishing like a scroll being rolled up"** may represent a mushroom-shaped cloud that is an after-effect of a tremendous nuclear blast.

It is possible that this "great earthquake" initiated by opening the "sixth seal" is the very same earthquake that will destroy the coalition of armies descending upon Israel in the great war described in Ezekiel 38-39.[1]

This 6th seal event may provide us with foresight as to the time of the coming "trumpet judgments."

[1] Ezekiel 38:19

Notes:

(Slide # 10)

THE OPENING OF THE SEVENTH SEAL

When the Lamb opened the seventh seal, there was silence in heaven for about half an hour. ***Revelation 8:1***

Key Points:

It appears that with the opening of this final seal, the entire prophetic Book of Revelation is opened for all to see.

- And when the Book of Revelation was opened to their understanding, they were speechless; for it reveals that the devastations that are released with the opening of the 6th seal is merely a glimpse of greater events to come.

This "seventh seal" has no plague or judgment content, but its opening actually launches the sounding of the seven trumpets. In summary:

- The first six seals relate to forces leading up to the time of that period known as the Great Tribulation,
- While the seven trumpets actually launch the beginning of these Great Tribulation events.

Notes:

(Slides # 11 & 12)

SILENCE IN HEAVEN AND THE PRAYERS OF THE SAINTS

(Revelation 8:1-5)

During this silence in heaven, seven angels are standing before the throne of God and they receive seven trumpets.

Key Points:

- They do not immediately commence blowing these trumpets, but they reverently keep silent until something else has been finished.
- Then another angel approaches the altar, receives incense along with the prayers of the saints, and then kindles the incense with the fire from the altar, he stands before the Throne of God and causes the incense and the prayers of the saints to ascend up to the Lord Almighty.
- It is very evident that the all-important elements to this period of silence are the prayers of the saints rising up before the Lord. What is the object of these prayers?

"Our Father, who art in heaven; blessed be thy Name; Thy kingdom come; Thy will be done upon earth as it is in heaven."

- This is the cry of God's beloved sons and daughters who have been calling for His Kingdom to come for more than four thousand years.

The time has now come for the launching of judgments that will prepare the world for the second coming of our Lord to set up His Kingdom across the entire earth. [2]

Then the angel took the censer and filled it with fire from the altar and threw it on the earth, and there were peals of thunder, rumblings, flashes of lightning, and an earthquake. ***Revelation 8:5***

Notes:

____

____

____

____

____

____

____

BREAK-TIME **(Slides # 13 - 14)**

[2] Herman Hoeksema. *Behold, He Cometh* (Grand Rapids, MI: Reformed Free Publishing Assn, 1969) p.296-297.

(Slides # 15 - 16)

THE SEVEN TRUMPETS – AN OVERVIEW

(Revelation 8:6-12)

Trumpets are used in Scripture to awaken people to matters of extreme importance or summon them to war against an approaching enemy.

Listen to the prophecy of Joel concerning this time:

Blow a trumpet in Zion; sound an alarm on my holy mountain! Let all the inhabitants of the land tremble, for the day of the LORD is coming; it is near, a day of darkness and gloom, a day of clouds and thick darkness! ***Joel 2:1-2***

Now there is a symbolic parallelism between the trumpet events that we are now addressing and the plagues that God rained down on Egypt in the days of Moses.

- Certainly, plagues from heaven could occur again within these trumpet series of events, but the symbolism of the devastations this trumpets series are very descriptive of a nuclear holocaust.
- Either way, the challenges which the world, as well as the church, will soon face will be just as difficult, if not worse than the chaotic events addressed in this session.
- Thus, I am using a nuclear scenario which will bring much clearer understanding of these devastating events for our 21st century culture.

Key Points:

It seems probable that the first six trumpet prophecies foretell all the major events that will occur in the aftermath of a single nuclear war - a war that destroys much of the environment as well as numerous human lives.

- Collectively, the first "six trumpets" document the ferocity of a nuclear war and the war's immediate aftermath.
- While the "7th trumpet" deals with ongoing, long-term repercussions following this nuclear war.

These seven trumpet plagues fall into two separate groups:

- The first four are directed against the elements of nature and the heavenlies.
- The last three, which are called "**woes**," show their effect upon mankind.

(Slides # 17 - 18)

The First Trumpet Sounds = A Burning of the Land

The first angel blew his trumpet, and there followed **hail** and **fire**, mixed with **blood**, and these were thrown upon the earth. And a third of the earth was burned up, and a third of the trees were burned up, and all green grass was burned up. ***Revelation 8:7***

Key Points:

Nuclear hail is formed when large quantities of earth and water are sucked into the fireball and become vaporized.

- They gradually descend to earth in what we call fallout. John appears to describe this nuclear fallout as hail since it does look like ordinary hailstones.
- The fallout of hail that falls quickly back to earth, within one day, is generally the size of a marble. Lighter particles continue to fall like dusty snow, and eventually invisibly, for weeks afterwards.
- This affects the food crops that are subjected to severe contamination and they cannot be harvested for decades.
- Now a single megaton bomb can set ninety-five square miles on fire at the same time – but this is so much more devastating.

"Mixed with blood" could possibly be vaporized remains of humans and animals falling back to earth following the blast.

- Those in the vicinity of an air-burst nuclear explosion would be instantly reduced to super-heated gases and would eventually fall to the earth as vaporized blood along with other burning debris.

Finally, note also the parallelism of the 1st trumpet with the 7th Egyptian plague during the days of Moses when thunder, heavy hail, and fire fell upon the land of Egypt.

- This hail struck down every plant of the field and broke every tree.
- Only in the land of Goshen, where the people of Israel were, was there no hail.

Notes:

(Slide # 19)

Second Trumpet Sounds = Burning of the Sea & Marine Life

The second angel blew his trumpet, and something like a great mountain, burning with fire, was thrown into the sea, and a third of the sea became blood. A third of the living creatures in the sea died, and a third of the ships were destroyed. ***Revelation 8:8-9***

Key Points:

- The great mountain burning with fire is not easy to identify. Some commentators believe that it may be a fiery meteor. This is certainly possible, but also this could well be the naval part of this war.
- Nuclear submarines will undoubtedly be part of this war and therefore, the naval vessels at sea will be under attack since that is where the large portion of nuclear weaponry is launched.
- Like the land masses, a one-third of the seas will be destroyed with much death.

Again, note also that the parallel of the 2nd trumpet with the 1st Egyptian plague during the days of Moses when the Egyptian waters were struck and turned into blood.[3]

(Slides # 20 - 21)

The Third Trumpet Sounds = A Burning of the Fresh Water

The third angel blew his trumpet, and a great star fell from heaven, blazing like a torch, and it fell on a third of the rivers and on the springs of water. The name of the star is **Wormwood**. A third of the waters became wormwood, and many people died from the water, because it had been made bitter. ***Revelation 8:10-11***

Key Points:

- Wormwood is a bitter herb that Scripture employs as a symbol of bitterness and sorrow which God gives to them who forsake Him.[4]
- Here it is probably used to describe extreme bitterness in the fresh waters caused by radioactive fallout. This certainly identifies the nuclear radiation effect upon the interior of the continents where the world's rivers and lakes are found.
- Drinking of poisonous waters will result in a slow, painful death from radiation sickness.
- Starting with nausea, vomiting, diarrhea, victims will experience internal bleeding, ulcerations of the lips, and loss of hair within 2 weeks.
- Many will undoubtedly die from these embittered waters.

[3] Exodus 7:20-21
[4] Jeremiah 9:15

Notes:

____

____

____

____

(Slide # 22)

The Fourth Trumpet Sounds = A Darkening of the Heavens

The fourth angel blew his trumpet, and a third of the sun was struck, and a third of the moon, and a third of the stars, so that a third of their light might be darkened, and a third of the day might be kept from shining, and likewise a third of the night. ***Revelation 8:12***

Key Points:

- The incineration of one-third of the earth will not be the result of a detonation of a few nuclear bombs. Even the ten kiloton atomic bomb dropped on Nagasaki in 1945 blocked the sun's rays for a short period of time.
- Once high altitude nuclear smoke clouds encircle the earth they will become a miles thick, dark curtain throughout the skies. These thick clouds will block the sun and the moon which will shorten the length of daylight as well as the night-lights.
- Studies of the post-effect of nuclear warfare reveal that the lands would experience sub-freezing temperatures over most of the northern hemisphere.
- These temperatures could remain below freezing for months resulting in a **severe "nuclear winter**."[5]

Note also the parallel of the 4th trumpet with the 9th Egyptian plague during the days of Moses which caused darkness throughout the land for three days. However, all the people of Israel had light where they lived.[6]

Notes:

____

____

____

____

[5] Charles W. Miller, *Today's Technology in Bible Prophecy* (Lansing, MI: TIP, 1990) p.178-182
[6] Exodus 10:20-23

(Slides # 23 - 24)

THE EAGLE'S WARNING – "WOE, WOE, WOE"

Key Points:

At the completion of events emanating from the first four trumpets, one-third of mankind's entire physical universe has been decimated.

- The land, the oceans, the lakes and rivers, and the skies have all suffered tremendous devastation. Sickness and epidemics from a poisoned environment will abound worldwide. However, it is about to get worse.

Suddenly, John is shown an eagle flying across the heavens and proclaiming that the next three trumpet judgments will be delivered directly against mankind rather than the environment:

> Then I looked, and I heard an eagle crying with a loud voice as it flew directly overhead, "Woe, woe, woe to those who dwell on the earth, at the blasts of the other trumpets that the three angels are about to blow!" ***Revelation 8:13***

Notes:

BREAK-TIME (Slides # 25 - 26)

(Slides # 27 & 28)

FIFTH TRUMPET WOE – LOCUSTS STINGING LIKE SCORPIONS

(Revelation 9:3-10)

Then from the smoke came locusts on the earth, and they were given power like the power of scorpions of the earth. They were told not to harm the grass of the earth or any green plant or any tree**, but only those people who do not have the seal of God on their foreheads**. They were allowed to torment them for five months, but not to kill them, and their torment was like the torment of a scorpion when it stings someone. ***Revelation 9:3-5***

Revelation 9:3-5 - Summary

- Then from the smoke came locusts on the earth, and
- They were given power like the power of scorpions of the earth.
- They were told not to harm the grass of the earth or any green plant or any tree,
- But only those people who do not have the seal of God on their foreheads.
- They were allowed to torment them for five months, but not to kill them,
- Their torment was like the torment of a scorpion when it stings someone.

Key Points:

Now, out of the aftermath of a nuclear strike, something will arise to attempt to control and then later - take advantage of this catastrophic situation:

The Bible has previously referred to locusts as vast destructive armies.[7] It is conceivable that these locusts are representative of a vast, perhaps global, military force.

Thus, our "fifth trumpet" scenario is designed to reveal what this event will look like from a worldly perspective in the twenty-first century.

- Which tells us that "locusts" are symbolic of a vast military force.

Notes:

____

____

____

____

[7] Judges 6:3-5

(Slide # 29)

FIFTH TRUMPET WOE - THE NEED FOR MARTIAL LAW

The typical survivor's first reaction to these events will be panic, but this will eventually be replaced by anger.

Key Points:

- There will undoubtedly be a huge outbreak of crime including robbery and murder, especially in the urban areas.
- Food and water will be scarce: supplies, transportation, fuel will be nonexistent. There will be a frantic hoarding of food; neighborhood homes will be attacked by gangs and small groups of criminal bands seeking food and other goods.
- This will eventually be organized by gang leadership who will recruit these bands to steal for them in order to gain items to sell on the black market.
- Crops will be highly valued for food and trees will be highly prized for heating, cooking, and building shelters.

Thus, martial law would be the initial measure taken by an existing government to protect the food supplies and to restore order among the survivors to insure their nation's survival.

Key Points:

- This army will not be sent to destroy, but to protect environmental property like the trees and crops that survived the nuclear strike.
- Their supposed mission is to establish law and order in those communities struggling to survive the chaotic aftermath of the nuclear war.
- Their initial orders are not to kill anyone which is a typical order given to combat troops sent to restore order during national emergencies.
- This command is important in preventing an armed revolt from arising among the masses. However, concentration camps will certainly be employed.

Notes:

(Slides # 30 & 31)

FIFTH TRUMPET WOE - THE APPEARANCE OF THE LOCUSTS

In appearance the locusts were like horses prepared for battle: on their **heads were what looked like crowns of gold**; their **faces were like human face**s, their hair like women's hair, and their **teeth like lions' teeth**; they had **breastplates like breastplates of iron**, and the **noise of their wings was like the noise of many chariots with horses rushing into battle**. ***Revelation 9:7-9***

The appearance of these "5th trumpet" locusts appear similar to helicopter gun-ship's which would certainly be utilized by this peace-keeping force.

Key Points:

- The "**crown" of rotor blades**, the **"faces of men" in the cockpit**, the **locust-shaped body of the chopper,** the **"lion's teeth" armament**; all this appears to identify the use of numerous helicopter gun-ship's, tanks, and vehicles to police the countryside and provide support for the ground troops, and to transport prisoners to concentration camps.
- The whirring noise of the rotor blades could be identified with the sound of **locust wings**
- The thump, thump, thump sound of a chopper passing overhead could be identified with **chariots of many horses running to battle.**
- Looking upward at whirling helicopter blades resemble a woman' dark hair blowing in the wind.

Notes:

(Slides # 32 thru 34)

FIFTH TRUMPET WOE - THE APPEARANCE OF THE LOCUSTS

They have tails and stings like scorpions, and their power to hurt people for five months is in their tails. ***Revelation 9:10***

Key Points:

What this is saying is that these military forces will be characteristic of a "scorpion army."

- Scorpions are so bad-tempered that they will lash out at anyone or anything that dare to cross their path. The weaponry used by this peace-keeping force will be like the tail of a scorpion.

- Although they were ordered not to kill the masses, they will certainly inflict pain and torment and thus, it appears as if **taser-gun weaponry** will be involved. This is weaponry that will inflict pain like a sting of a scorpion, but will not cause death.

The "sealed ones" of God will be exempt from being harmed by this force.

Notes:

____

____

____

____

(Slide # 35)

FIFTH TRUMPET WOE – NUCLEAR WINTER

They were allowed **to torment them for five months**, but not to kill them, and their torment was like the torment of a scorpion when it stings someone. And in those days people will seek death and will not find it. They will long to die, but death will flee from them. ***Revelation 9:5-6***

These peace-keeping efforts will last for five months which seems to coincide with the length of a nuclear winter; a period of time when temperatures are below freezing and a third of the light from the sun and moon has been darkened.

Key Points:

- Tests reveal that in a ten thousand-megaton yield exchange, which is enough firepower to burn up a third of the earth, sub-freezing temperatures could last almost six months.

- John is describing five months of wide-spread famine and political upheaval in the midst of arctic-type temperatures; a period of time of such grief and hopelessness for the world citizenry that many will seek death, but death will flee from them and they will have to continue in their deep suffering for a time. [8]

Five dreadful months is emphasized: Why?

- It would be wise to make the preparations and commitment necessary to survive a nuclear winter. We definitely should store up food and water and other provisions that will last for at least, five months during a time of freezing weather.

Notes:

(Slide # 36)

FIFTH TRUMPET WOE – THE ARRIVAL OF APOLLYON

They have as king over them the angel of the bottomless pit. His name in Hebrew is Abaddon, and in Greek he is called Apollyon. ***Revelation 9:11***

- Both Abaddon and Apollyon means "**destruction**" or "**to destroy**".

Key Points:

Here we are introduced to the global commander over this so-called peace-keeping force.

- The reference to this "**king" being the "angel of the bottomless pit**" describes this world leader's dark character and mission.

[8] Charles W. Miller, *Today's Technology in Bible Prophecy* (Lansing, MI: TIP, 1990) p.196-213

- **His name exposes this demonically empowered leader's evil character and hidden agenda**. (The word for "angel" in this verse could also be interpreted as "messenger)."
- Perhaps this is the coming world leader who will be claiming that his mission is to bring about world-wide peace. He will certainly be welcomed among the masses that have survived this nuclear war.
- If this is the Antichrist who is yet to be revealed, he will need the backing of the world's military establishment as his first step for world power.

Notes:

____
____
____
____
____
____
____
____
____
____
____
____

BREAK-TIME (Slides # 37 - 38)

(Slides # 39 thru 41)

SIXTH TRUMPET WOE – A 200 MILLION DEMONIC ARMY

(Revelation 9:13-21)

Key Points:

With the sounding of the sixth trumpet, demonic forces are released that will mobilize a murderous "demonic" army numbering 200 million with a mission of killing approximately two billion of the world's inhabitants.

- Many commentators believe this to be an organized army from the east, perhaps from China, that rises up out of the turmoil in order to conquer and control the remainder of the earth.
- Another possibility: Cells of organized Islamic terrorists, who reside in countries around the world, may believe that this long-awaited "great earthquake" launches the coming of their Mahdi, and thus they may launch a worldwide war for their god, Allah.

Key Points to Consider:

However - Do these terrorists really number 200 million? Think about this: - The actual number of men composing this murderous army may be far less than 200 million.

- This vision describes 200 million demonic horsemen. It is quite possible that these are actual demons which possess members of a smaller size army of Muslim terrorists.
- Remember the "legion" of demons that possessed one man that Jesus released into a herd of pigs – they were 2,000 demons within the soul of that one man.[9]
- Likewise, it could be that similar demonic "legions" occupy each member of a terrorist army with a tremendous murderous agenda. (Perhaps a 100,000 man army possessed by 200 million demons.).
- This may also be a time of destruction of Islamic terrorism.

Notes:

____

____

____

(Slides # 42 & 43)

SIXTH TRUMPET WOE – A 200 MILLION DEMONIC ARMY

(Revelation 9:13-21)

Regardless of the identity of this army which will kill one-third of mankind, it does have the characteristics of a nuclear onslaught:

And this is how I saw the horses in my vision and those who rode them: they wore breastplates the color of fire and of sapphire and of sulfur, and the heads of the horses were like lions' heads, and **fire** and **smoke** and **sulfur** came out of their mouths. ***Revelation 9:17***

Key Points:

The three plagues of fire, smoke, and sulfur certainly sound like the three devastating effects of nuclear devices. For example:

- Fire = Blast from being in proximity of explosion.
- Smoke = A visible manifestation of heat which travels much further out then the blast
- Sulfur = Radiation which travels great distances from the initial explosion.

This certainly appears to describe a nuclear war that kills 1/3 of the world's population.

---

[9] Mark 5:1-13

Consider this Scenario of the Trumpet Series:

If the trumpet series is indeed nuclear as previously described, and a third of the earth will be destroyed or polluted, then surely it will result in a tremendous loss of lives which may be included within the "6th trumpet" scenario.

If this is correct, then the six trumpets that sounded are not successive but symbolic of the respective devastations that occur in the different elements of the earth following a world-wide nuclear war. That is, how the nuclear war devastates the land, the seas, the fresh water, the atmosphere, and its effect upon mankind.

One can only speculate concerning the specifics of this destructive scenario; however it is a certainty that these plagues are a supernatural force led by the four demonic angels who have been waiting for centuries for this murderous opportunity to unleash their hatred against humanity.

- A very clear description of this breathtaking demonic army and its destructive intent is very similar to what is also described by the prophets, Joel and Isaiah.[10]

Notes:

(Slides # 44 thru 47)

THE TRUMPET SERIES – ITS EFFECT UPON MANKIND

Key Points:

These devastating events are obviously punitive in nature, but they are also intended to bring many to repentance.

- Yet the great majority of the world's population will not repent. They may even be more deeply embittered toward God and the church, who they will blame for the devastation.

- However, like the Israelites who were protected against the plagues that came upon their Egyptian captors, those who are sealed will also be protected.

[10] Joel 2:1-11 and Isaiah 24:1-15

- Nevertheless, they too will be indirectly affected by these plagues, as hardships abound worldwide and unsealed members of their family and friends become victims.

- Yet, the ones who are "sealed" will not fear and will continually praise the Lord in their circumstances.[11]

As a result, the light of Jesus will shine mightily through them which will create an astounding, dual effect upon mankind.

- That is, many will repent and turn to the Lord who will protect and provide for them.
- But the large majority will be more deeply embittered toward God and the church, who they will blame for the devastation.

Much fear and confusion will be present among the majority of the Christian world throughout this period of the trumpets.

- Such gloom and doubt will cause many to begin to lose sight of their Lord and His revelation as they begin to cry out, "Why does God allow this to happen?"

It is at this point that John witnesses the coming of a mighty angel into the midst of this devastation who will equip His army for upcoming events.

Notes:

____

____

____

BREAK-TIME (Slides # 48 & 49)

(Slide # 50)

A MIGHTY ANGEL BRINGS A LITTLE BOOK

(Revelation 10:1-11)

Here we have the symbolic significance of the preparation of John and every true witness of Christ in the world as a prophet. The message that he was to bring was not going to be sweet to the taste of the world, but one of tremendous difficulty and sorrow and judgment.

- Because of this it will be contradicted and opposed, not only by the wicked world of Antichrist but also by much of the church as it currently exists.

[11] Psalm 23; Job 1:21

- For many who do not truly belong to Christ but are in the church will hate and deny and oppose the message of tribulation and judgment. They will shout "Peace, peace when there is no peace."[12]

- It may also be opposed by many of the true people of God; those who do not always see and understand that in this world the church must expect tribulation and judgment in order for the kingdom to come. Tribulation brings separation between God's people & the world's.

- It takes spiritual courage, the courage of a warrior with great faith, to be a messenger during these times. And in order to stand against this opposition, the prophet of this message must **"eat" the book** of this prophecy.

It must become part of their very being.

(Slides # 51 & 52)

A MIGHTY ANGEL BRINGS A LITTLE BOOK

(Revelation 10:1-11)

What is the content of this book?

It appears to be the message of the Seventh Trumpet. A message revealing:

(1) Severe battles, destruction, persecution and vengeance
(2) The fate of Jerusalem and the temple
(3) The ministry and fate of the two witnesses who are killed for their testimony
(4) The conflict between Woman and Dragon who attempts to destroy her Child
(5) The Beast which arises out of the sea and the Beast that arises out of the earth
(6) The overwhelming power of Antichrist and his war upon the people of God
(7) Tribulation and oppression for the sake of Christ's kingdom
(8) Mystery Babylon and her greatness as well as her destruction

A MIGHTY ANGEL BRINGS A LITTLE BOOK

(Revelation 10:1-11)

It appears to be the message of the Seventh Trumpet. A message revealing:

(9) The pouring out of seven vials of wrath which devastate the entire earth
(10) The coming of the Lord Jesus with his army of holy warriors
(11) The establishment of a millennial kingdom on this earth
(12) The binding and subsequent loosing of Satan
(13) The great Day of Judgment before the Throne of our Lord
(14) The coming down from heaven of the new Jerusalem
(15) The restoration of new heavens and new earth where righteousness reigns forever

[12] Jeremiah 6:14

Thus, this little book contains a tremendous, terrible message that has a glorious finale, at least for the people of God.

(Slide # 53)

A MIGHTY ANGEL BRINGS A LITTLE BOOK
(Revelation 10:1-11)

He also provides His 'witnesses" with their mission assignment:

- **That is, this little book must not be merely read; it must be eaten!**

The prophet Ezekiel had a very similar experience for he also had to "eat" the scroll before he was prepared to proclaim God's message of tribulation and mourning upon the house of Israel.

➢ He was told that the house of Israel is stiff necked and rebellious, so he must expect opposition, **and in order to stand for the Lord with this message, it must be part of his very system.**[13]

Notes:

____

____

____

____

____

(Slides # 54 & 55)

WARRIORS OF THE MESSAGE MUST "EAT THIS BOOK"

If John had simply read the little book, its contents would have still remained outside of him and would not have influenced his heart and mind.

➢ Thus, he would not have been a strong prophet of this message who could passionately stand for the truth of God in the midst of opposition and suffering and tribulation.

Key Points:

The message of this book:

➢ Must become part of his flesh and blood, his soul and spirit.
➢ Must transform him, change him, and make a different man out of him.

[13] Ezekiel 2:8 through 3:3

- Its truth must so dominate him that he can never believe anything else and can never be silenced about it.

Now, this was not merely revealed to John, so that the passage would have no significance for us. It teaches what we must do with the testimony of God in general, but especially with the Book of Revelation.

- We can study the book and listen to various interpretations and we might find intellectual enjoyment in its interpretation. Perhaps our curiosity is somewhat satisfied, but that is not sufficient. **The message of this book demands a positive stand.**

The question is: Do we believe these things? Is it really true that:

- The world is in iniquity and will fight to the last against Christ and His kingdom?
- There is an apostate part of the church which will align itself with the Antichrist?
- That the kingdom of Christ will come in no other way except through world wide wars, judgments, and tribulations?

If you believe these things, the book of this prophecy will determine your stand against the world and prepare you for opposition within the church and for a great falling away.

Are you ready?

- If so, you must eat it, appropriate it; it must become part of your entire system and control the direction of your life, so that you only know one life, the Kingdom of God.

Blessed is the one who reads aloud the words of this prophecy, and blessed are those who hear, and who keep what is written in it, for the time is near. ***Revelation 1:3***

(Slide # 56)

WARRIORS OF THE MESSAGE MUST "EAT THIS BOOK"

Key Points:

The little book speaks of joy, peace, and everlasting life, but it also speaks many woes and tribulations.

- Commitment to "eat" this little book does not mean that the Word of God has no bitter after-effects when it reaches the belly.

- The process of assimilation and digestion is often painful for the Word of God has to battle against the influence of the flesh and its lusts; and this battle, however sweet it was when first eaten, is a painful one.

- It causes bitterness and struggle until the medicine of the Word of God has done its work and transformed us.

This is especially true in the book of Revelation for this little book speaks of redemption, salvation, heavenly glory, and a new creation where our tears are wiped away, of highest joy and eternal life.

- This is the also the popular, continuing message of the church. **But**, the little book speaks of this only after self-denial and suffering and great personal sacrifice has occurred.

- The eating of this book is not simply studying and reading it; but it requires continuous fasting and praying for spiritual insight - for a life of continuous prayer and fasting is needed for those who desire to be prophetic messengers.

- It holds before us the glory of the future, **but** only at the end of a dark and challenging road to travel. This is not a popular message in most of today's churches.

Notes – Consider the changes & self-discipline that is required to "eat" this little book.

____

____

____

____

____

(Slides # 57 & 58)

WARRIORS OF THE MESSAGE MUST "EAT THIS BOOK"

Key Points:

It is a road of battle for the Kingdom of God. It is a road of persecution and mockery on the part of the world.

Suffering As a Christian
Beloved, do not be surprised at the **fiery trial** when it comes upon you to test you, as though something strange were happening to you. But rejoice insofar as you share Christ's sufferings, that you may also rejoice and be glad when his glory is revealed. ***1 Peter 4:12-13***

Jesus Himself tells us, "He that shall save his life will lose it, but he that shall lose his life for My sake shall save it."

- That is hard. That is not according to the flesh, but as it begins its work of transformation, the truth of the book may at first seem painful as it mortifies the old man, but more and more leave nothing but one desire, the coming Kingdom of God. [14]

This should be the effect of our assimilating this little book of prophecy.

[14] Herman Hoeksema. *Behold, He Cometh* (Grand Rapids, MI: Reformed Free Publishing Association, 1969) c.23

Notes:

(Slide # 59)

GOD'S MIGHTY WARRIORS WILL ARISE TO GUIDE MANY INTO THE KINGDOM

Key Points:

The time is rapidly approaching when warrior-type leaders, many of whom are outside the traditional American church, will need to network with one another in order to stand together and confront the dark challenges that await this generation.

This is a time:

- When numerous disciples of the Lord Jesus, like Peter, Paul, and John, will arise from among His prepared remnant to lead His people toward their respective callings.
- When many true prophets, like Ezekiel, Jeremiah, and Zechariah will also arise to provide understanding and direction to those with ears to hear.

These are the 144,000 that have been sealed prior to the sounding of the trumpet judgments.

Notes:

(Slide # 60)

THE NEXT SESSION:

First Read: Revelation 11

WARRIORS FOR CHRIST IN THE MIDST OF GREAT TRIBULATION

- A Graphic Picture of the Church in the End-Times Generation
- Identifying the Temple & the Holy City
- Measuring the Temple – What Does That Mean?
- Inhabitants of the Temple & the Holy City
- Identity of the Two Witnesses Ministering in Tribulation
- The Two Witnesses and their Gospel Message
- The Power of "Two by Two"
- A Second Resurrection Following the Final Gospel Proclamation
- The Events that Occur at the Sounding of the Seventh Trumpet

Additional Notes:

THE LAMB OF GOD - OUR TRUE "COMMANDER-IN-CHIEF"

The days are rapidly approaching when a tremendous separation will take place among mankind.

Yet, during this present era of warfare, He reigns as our Commander-in-Chief and His Name continues to be the battle cry for those warriors who fight daily for righteousness and truth.

His name is Jesus, Our Lord, Our King, Our Commander-in-Chief

- **A truly mighty Leader who would never delegate assignments to His people that He Himself wouldn't readily embrace.**
- **A Commander that Christian warriors will readily follow not matter the danger or what costs have to be paid.**
- **These are warriors whose deepest desire is to hear Jesus welcome them with the following words when they enter into His presence:**

.... 'Well done, good and faithful servant. You have been faithful over a little; I will set you over much. Enter into the joy of your master.' ***Matthew 25:21***

WARRIORS FOR CHRIST
IN THE MIDST OF
GREAT TRIBULATION

(Revelation 11)

SESSION #7 – WORKBOOK
Intended For
"KINGDOM WARRIORS IN THE ARMY OF GOD"

Unveiling Mysteries in the "Book of Revelation"

Based upon the Book:

GOD'S ANOINTED WARRIORS

By

Dr. Donald Bell
Major USMC, Ret.

(Slides # 2 - 3)

Introduction:

Spiritual insight into the events recorded in chapter 11 of the Book of Revelation is essential for leadership in the Army of God if we are to have a foundational understanding of our role within an evil world system --- A system that is committed to erasing the name of Jesus Christ from the earth and establishing its own eternal kingdom.

Now - In this chapter we are presented with:

- A graphic picture of the church in the end-times generation.
- The identity of God's Anointed "Witnesses"
- An overview of the battles to be fought during this time.
- A powerful gospel message that the Lord's chosen people will take throughout the earth.
- Several truths that Jesus taught concerning the events that will precede His 2nd coming.

It is important to remember that the Book of Revelation has been written to the church in order to provide understanding of coming events so that Christian leadership will be equipped to lead the Lord's people through these tremendously challenging battles which lie before us.

(Slides # 4 - 5)

THE TEMPLE AND THE HOLY CITY

Then I was given a measuring rod like a staff, and I was told, "Rise and measure the **temple of God and the altar** and those who worship there, but do not measure the **court outside the temple**; leave that out, for it is given over to the nations, and they will trample the **holy city** for forty-two months. ***Revelation 11:1-2***

Key Points:

There are three significant areas being addressed here:

- First, there is **the temple which includes the altar** where the people of God gather together to worship their Lord.

- Secondly, there is **the outer court** which is that area that surrounds the temple and where many gather together, but do not enter the temple itself.

- Finally, there is the **holy city** which, together with the outer court, will be surrendered to the world's forces for a period of 42 months (1,260 days).

Now, regarding these three separate areas, John is commanded to measure only the temple with the altar and those who worship within.

(Slide # 6)

THE TEMPLE AND THE HOLY CITY

Key Points:

Passages in the New Testament clearly reveal that the **"Temple of God"** is a spiritual structure composed of every true "born again" Christian. [15]

- Jesus Himself is also part of this spiritual temple for He is the "cornerstone" upon which the entire temple is built. [16]
- The ancient prophets and apostles of the Lord are also described as being the foundation of this temple.
- Therefore, it should be apparent that it is **YOU, the church** that is in view when this text speaks of the temple and the holy city.
- This temple has been continually growing through the centuries as believers have entered into the Kingdom of God.
- However, this holy Temple of God will not be completed until the gospel of Christ has gone out to the peoples of all the nations around the globe;[17] its completion appears to be finished at the time of the sounding of the seventh trumpet.[18]
- There is nothing more holy to the Lord than this spiritual temple and all who attempt to destroy it, will themselves be destroyed. [19]

Notes:

[15] 2 Corinthians 6:16
[16] Matthew 21:42; Ephesians 2:20
[17] Matthew 24:14
[18] Revelation 11:15-19
[19] 1 Corinthians 3:16-17; Ephesians 2:19-22

(Slides # 7 - 8)

THE TEMPLE AND THE HOLY CITY

Key Points:

This spiritual temple resides in the "holy city" which is also a spiritual city whose inhabitants are all those who profess the God of Israel to be their God.

- In fact, Jesus Christ Himself has also been called the "City of the Lord."[20]
- Yet within this city resides many rebellious citizens who confess the Lord, but do not live in righteousness:

"Listen to this, O house of Jacob, you who are called by the name of Israel and come from the line of Judah, you who take oaths in the name of the Lord and invoke the God of Israel — but not in truth or righteousness — you who call yourselves citizens of the holy city and rely on the God of Israel — the Lord Almighty is his name. ***Isaiah 48:1-2 (NIV)***

- Here the Lord admonishes the faithless hypocrites among his chosen people.
- These seemingly pious Israelites practiced idol-worship & temple prostitution on the side and yet pretended that they were true citizens of his holy city.

Key Points:

Recognize the parallelism here: just as many of the ancient citizens of Jerusalem were supposedly inhabitants of the city of God, so also the spiritual Jerusalem of this dispensation is inhabited by nominal Christians.

We need to understand that the "holy city" described in this text is representative of the entire world of Christianity; that is, all who have been baptized in the name of Jesus.

Notes:

[20] Isaiah 60:14

(Slides # 9 thru 12)

INHABITANTS OF THE TEMPLE AND THE HOLY CITY

The temple and the holy city described in these verses is the contemporary church of the end-times generation and the altar of atonement within the temple represents the person of Jesus Christ which is that place where God's people are redeemed within the holy city.

Therefore, within this "Holy City" are three broad classes of Christianity:

1. **There is a segment of the church that stays within the "holy city."**

- This is a church that proclaims belief in Christianity but will not truly profess Jesus Christ as the true Son of God and the one and only way to eternal life. To them Christianity is simply one of many religions that worship the same God.
- This is the false church, similar to those in ancient Jerusalem who continued to worship their man-made theology. **This is a city serving the purposes of Satan.**

2. **There is also a segment of the church that resides in the outer court.**

- These are the tares among the wheat; they go with God's people to His temple for worship, but they never enter that spiritual sanctuary of fellowship with God.
- They represent the "show church"; that part of Christianity which outwardly pretends to belong to the true church. They are not truly repentant since they will not forsake their worldly habits and simply profess Jesus as their fire insurance policy that will get them into heaven.
- They are invited into the temple, but they choose to remain in the outer court. They love to attend the churches in Sardis, Ephesus, and Laodicea. This is where the money-changers hang out. This is also where they are not confronted with their secret, sinful lifestyle.

For the time is coming when people will not endure sound teaching, but having itching ears they will accumulate for themselves teachers to suit their own passions, and will turn away from listening to the truth and wander off into myths. ***2 Timothy 4:3-4***

3. **Finally, within the temple reside the true people of God who worship at the altar of Christ in spirit and in truth.**

- These are those who have truly committed their life to the Lord and are frequently found in their prayer closets alone with God.
- They have a heart burdened for justice, righteousness, and integrity and they long to see the name of Jesus Christ glorified throughout the earth.
- They also have a heart deeply burdened for those who stay in the "outer court" and in the "city proper."
- Although their words may sound somewhat harsh and cruel to many, they are meant to awaken righteousness among those residing outside the temple.

Just as there were three distinctions in old Jerusalem: <u>the city proper</u>, <u>the outer court</u>, and finally <u>the temple</u>.

- So there are three distinctions in spiritual Jerusalem of our day:
- The Christian world includes the <u>false church</u>, the <u>show-church</u>, and the <u>true church of God</u>.

Notes:

____

____

____

____

____

____

____

____

(Slide # 13)

A TRUE PHYSICAL TEMPLE WILL AGAIN BE BUILT IN JERUSALEM

Finally, I do want to emphasize that a new physical temple will soon be built by the Jewish citizens of physical Jerusalem, which will definitely be a sign of the times.

<u>Key Points:</u>

- The building of this temple will probably take place following the victory of God's people in the Middle Eastern war described earlier in the sixth seal event.
- While Israel is rebuilding their temple, the Lord will be in the process of completing the building of His temple; a spiritual temple made without hands in the hearts of His people.
- Thus, as we observe these things occurring throughout the world, we need to be able to discern what is simultaneously occurring in the spiritual and to be fully prepared to recognize all that will soon follow.

Notes:

____

____

____

____

(Slide # 14)

MEASURING THE TEMPLE

Now John was commissioned by the Lord to measure only the temple and not the outer court nor the holy city.

Key Points:

This is a spiritual act of separating the true church from the false.

- Here we are taught in symbolic language not only the condition of Christianity within this generation but also, how it will undoubtedly manifest itself as the end of the age approaches.

- Those who remain outside the temple will eventually reveal themselves as enemies of Christ and His true church.

When Jesus was teaching His disciples concerning the time of the end which precedes His 2nd coming, He says:

And Jesus answered them,

- *"See that no one leads you astray. For many will come in my name, saying, 'I am the Christ,' and they will lead many astray.*

And you will hear of wars and rumors of wars. See that you are not alarmed, for this must take place, but the end is not yet. For nation (ethnos) will rise against nation (ethnos), and kingdom against kingdom, and there will be famines and earthquakes in various places. All these are but the beginning of the birth pains.

"Then they will deliver you up to tribulation and put you to death, and you will be hated by all nations for my name's sake.

- *And then many will fall away and betray one another and hate one another.*
- *And many false prophets will arise and lead many astray.*
- *And because lawlessness will be increased, the love of many will grow cold.*
- *But the one who endures to the end will be saved.*

And this gospel of the kingdom will be proclaimed throughout the whole world as a testimony to all nations, and then the end will come. ***Matthew 24:4-14***

Now within the context of measuring the temple, John is told that two witnesses of the Lord would prophesy for 3 ½ years.

- This is also a designated time for the Antichrist to begin to exercise his authority upon the earth.[21]

BREAK-TIME (Slides # 15 - 16)

[21] Revelation 13:5-7

(Slides # 17 - 19)

THE TWO WITNESSES

I will grant authority to my **two witnesses**, and they will prophesy for 1,260 days, clothed in sackcloth." ***Revelation 11:3***

Key Points:

The identity of these two witnesses is one of the more controversial and difficult questions in this section of Revelation.

- Many modern interpreters believe them to be Moses (or perhaps Enoch) and Elijah who shall literally return to earth to fulfill their ministerial calling and then be killed by the Antichrist.
- This interpretation does possess an element of truth, and perhaps this is a possibility but it also limits our understanding of this passage if we think that it literally refers to two men.
- Moses and Elijah were great witnesses of the Lord in their day and as such, they should be viewed as stereotypes of those who will be called to proclaim a powerful gospel message in the coming days.
- Scripture reveals numerous champions of the Lord who stood strong for Him throughout their life on earth but, their earthly mission has been accomplished and now they reside eternally with the Lord.
- Other witnesses will soon arise to be anointed by the Lord to proclaim a great and powerful gospel message to the world in the coming days.

Many believe that the two witnesses in this text are not two single persons for they have universal influence throughout the entire world, and they are also universally hated and their eventual death brings universal joy among all the citizens of the world's kingdom.

- It is certainly not conceivable that two single individuals in a single city could cause so much commotion throughout the world. **Then who are these two witnesses**?

These are the **two olive trees and the two lampstands** that stand before the Lord of the earth. ***Revelation 11:4***

Notes:

(Slide # 20)

TWO OLIVE TREES AND TWO LAMPSTANDS

The reference to two olive trees and two lampstands refers back to a similar vision given to the prophet Zechariah centuries earlier.[22]

Key Points:

Zechariah received a vision from an angel of the Lord where he sees a candlestick containing seven lamps.

- Above the candlestick he sees a golden bowl filled with oil which provides each lamp with the oil needed to give light.
- Now on each side of this oil-filled bowl stood an olive tree; these two olive trees were the source of oil supplied to the golden bowl which then passed it on to the seven lamps.
- Thus, we have a candlestick receiving its oil from a bowl above it, which in turn receives its oil from the two olive trees.
- If the candlesticks, which are representative of the Christian church,[23] are to give true light, then oil must be provided by the two olive trees.

These olive trees are symbolic of the Holy Spirit of God who provides the oil of knowledge necessary to allow the light to shine through the people of God.

In summary, what John is seeing is symbolic of God's chosen disciples as they minister in the in the power of the Holy Spirit.

Notes:

[22] Zechariah 4
[23] Revelation 1:20

(Slides # 21 - 22)

THE POWER OF "TWO BY TWO"

It is always the testimony of two which must confirm the Word of God:

If I alone bear witness about myself, my testimony is not deemed true. There is another who bears witness about me, and I know that the testimony that he bears about me is true. You sent to John, and he has borne witness to the truth. ***John 5:31-33***

Jesus is always present wherever two or more are gathered together in His name:

Again I say to you, if two of you agree on earth about anything they ask, it will be done for them by my Father in heaven. For where two or three are gathered in my name, there am I among them." ***Matthew 18:19-20***

When Jesus dispatches His chosen ones to minister among the masses in His authority, it is always two by two.

Jesus Sends Out the Apostles

And he called the twelve and began to **send them out two by two, and gave them authority over the unclean spirits** …………And if any place will not receive you and they will not listen to you, when you leave, shake off the dust that is on your feet as a testimony against them." **So they went out and proclaimed that people should repent.** ***Mark 6:7-12***

Later, Jesus Sends Out the Seventy-Two

After this the Lord appointed seventy-two others and sent them on ahead of him, **two by two**, into every town and place where he himself was about to go. And he said to them, "The harvest is plentiful, but the laborers are few. Therefore pray earnestly to the Lord of the harvest to send out laborers into his harvest. Go your way; behold, **I am sending you out as lambs in the midst of wolves.** Carry no moneybag, no knapsack, no sandals, and greet no one on the road. Whatever house you enter, first say, 'Peace be to this house!' And if a son of peace is there, your peace will rest upon him. But if not, it will return to you…………….. **Heal the sick in it and say to them, 'The kingdom of God has come near to you.'**……..............**"The one who hears you hears me, and the one who rejects you rejects me, and the one who rejects me rejects him who sent me.**" ***Luke 10:1-16***

These are the Christians sent out onto the battlefield "Two by Two"

- Going to war for the Kingdom of God is very different than going into Afghanistan, Iraq or Vietnam. Soldiers in the Army of God are fighting to save people, not kill them.

- God's warrior soldiers are fighting to help free and save many of the very ones who will be used to fight against them. **These are hard truths that require continuing spiritual insight**.

(Slide # 23)

IDENTITY OF THE TWO WITNESSES IN MIDST OF GREAT TRIBULATION

Just as Jesus dispatched His chosen disciples two by two throughout the land of Israel, so He will again send out His disciples of this last generation two by two throughout the entire world.

Key Points:

- It is highly probable that these end-times disciples are the 144,000 (witnessing two by two), who were sealed prior to the sounding of the trumpet judgments.
- If so, their ministry begins during the coming "trumpet judgments" for they are sealed by the Lord during this period of time.

In Revelation 14, we see them gathered together with their Commander-in-Chief on Mount Zion. They are the firstfruits of God's people and they follow His Son wherever He goes.[24]

These 144,000 who have been sealed with the name of God on their foreheads come from far countries all around the world, but they will be gathered together with their Lord on Mount Zion.

- Perhaps this is a literal gathering prior to being sent out two by two throughout the earth; or perhaps it is a spiritual gathering with their Lord as He speaks to them individually within their hearts.

This is the time when His chosen vessels will minister in even greater power than was witnessed in the ministry of Jesus Christ during His 3 ½ year ministry 2,000 years ago:

> "Truly, truly, I say to you, whoever believes in me will also do the works that I do; and **greater works than these will he do, because I am going to the Father**. Whatever you ask in my name, this I will do, that the Father may be glorified in the Son. If you ask me anything in my name, I will do it. ***John 14:12-14***

The two witnesses (144,000) are like:

> Those who trust in the Lord are like Mount Zion, which cannot be moved, but abides forever.
> As the mountains surround Jerusalem, so the Lord surrounds his people, from this time forth and forevermore. **Psalms 125:1-2**

BREAK-TIME (Slides # 24 - 25)

[24] Revelation 14:1-5

(Slides # 26 thru 29)

THE TWO WITNESSES – THEIR MINISTRY

Their power over people and the environment will be like that reflected in the ministries of Moses and Elijah.

The gospel message of these 144,000 witnesses will reach every nation and people upon the earth. They are also described as being clothed in **"sackcloth" which denotes that their message will primarily be a call for repentance from sin.**

Go therefore and make disciples of all nations, baptizing them in the name of the Father and of the Son and of the Holy Spirit, ***Matthew 28:19***

And this gospel of the kingdom will be proclaimed throughout the whole world as a testimony to all nations, **and then the end will come**. ***Matthew 24:14***

The glory that you have given me I have given to them, that they may be one even as we are one, I in them and you in me, that they may become perfectly one, so that the world may know that you sent me and loved them even as you loved me. ***John 17:22-23***

They will go forth in the fullness of the tremendous glory of the Son of God during a time when worldwide technology and transportation will allow all inhabitants of the earth an opportunity to respond.

Daniel's Vision of the Time of the End:

And those who are wise shall shine like the brightness of the sky above; and those who turn many to righteousness, like the stars forever and ever. ---------- **Many shall run to and fro, and knowledge shall increase."** ***Daniel 12:3-4***

Notes:

(Slide # 30)

144,000 WILL REPRESENT THE "THIRD COMING" OF ELIJAH

Approximately 430 years before Christ, The Lord told the prophet Malachi:

"Behold, I will send you Elijah the prophet before the great and awesome day of the LORD comes.
Malachi 4:5

Key Points:

The Jewish religious community of today continues to await the return of Elijah seeing it as a sign preceding the coming of their Messiah.

- They believe it to be the literal physical presence of Elijah rather than one coming in the spirit of Elijah.
- However, the New Testament shows that it was John the Baptist who came in the spirit of Elijah for the purpose of "preparing the way of the Lord".[25]

As previously shown, the spirit and power of Elijah is also found to be present within the two witnesses.

- Therefore, as John the Baptist was anointed by God to call the people to repentance and to declare the coming of the Lord, it appears as if many with the anointing of Elijah, who are commissioned to call people from among all the nations to repentance, shall also be the voice of one crying in the wilderness, **"Prepare the way (for the 2nd coming) of the Lord; make His paths straight."**[26]

Like John, they too will be rejected by the religious leaders and sent instead to the poor, and the outcasts, who will hear the true words of God in the midst of tribulation. However, it will not be just one voice this time.[27]

Notes:

---

[25] Like 1:17; Matthew 11:14

[26] Matthew 3:3 (emphasis mine)

[27] Benjamin Baruch, *The Day of the Lord is at Hand* (Baruch Publishing, 2004) p.48

(Slide # 31)

THE GOSPEL MESSAGE OF THE TWO WITNESSES

The two witnesses of Christ who are the "sealed 144,000" will boldly and fearlessly stand united against the darkness of this age as they bear the testimony of Jesus Christ and His truth among all the nations of the earth.[28]

Key Points:

As to the contents of their message, this army of "two witnesses" will speak nothing but that which their Lord has commissioned them to speak.

- They will speak of Christ and His atoning blood which is the witness of the righteousness and holiness of God in the midst of a sinful world.
- They will openly condemn all efforts to seek salvation outside of that atoning blood which will infuriate the false church together with a worldly leadership that is attempting to establish a one world kingdom.
- This will be a time of tremendous miracles as the gospel message goes forth in a power greater than the world has ever seen; a time when the blind will see, the deaf will hear, and many of the afflicted will be healed throughout the world.[29]

Yet, it will also be a time when waters turn to blood, the skies are shut so no rain may fall, and plagues strike throughout the earth. The kingdom must come through tribulation and through all kinds of plagues and calamities.

- Do not think that this is strange; Moses delivered his people from Egypt by bringing great devastating plagues upon the land that brought Egypt to its knees.
- During Elijah's day the kingdom was again strengthened when he prayed that God would withhold rain for three years from an apostate nation.

Notes:

____

____

____

____

____

____

[28] Matthew 24:14
[29] John 14:12

(Slide # 32)

THE GOSPEL MESSAGE OF THE TWO WITNESSES

Key Points:

The mission of these end-times witnesses for Christ is not to bring peace to the world, but to bring division among the peoples.

- This is a hard teaching that is never heard from the pulpits, but separation has to take place.
- The pure light of holiness will not compromise with darkness. There can be no middle ground in the Kingdom of God.
- This truth of God is 180 degrees opposite that which is embraced by the worldly system which emphasizes "tolerance" as a requirement for world peace.
- Not surprisingly, the world's government will once again unite with the false church of Christianity to persecute the true church with the objective of erasing the hard gospel message of Jesus Christ from the earth.[30]

This will be a time of great tribulation never before seen since the creation of the earth yet, this will also be a time of a great harvest of souls such as the world has never before seen.

- There will be no more grey area; either one stands with Christ or against Him.
- Love and hatred will be clearly visible among all the inhabitants of the earth.

If we keep our eyes upon the Lord, our attitude in the midst of persecution and suffering will be one of great joy knowing that the eternal rewards that await us will be great.[31]

The following verse will be ongoing in their hearts:

"Blessed are you when others revile you and persecute you and utter all kinds of evil against you falsely on my account. Rejoice and be glad, for your reward is great in heaven, for so they persecuted the prophets who were before you. ***Matthew 5:11-12***

Notes:

[30] John 15:20; Matthew 24:10
[31] Matthew 5:10-12

(Slides # 33 - 34)

THE GOSPEL MESSAGE OF THE TWO WITNESSES

They will strongly proclaim the following truths:

1. **Jesus Christ is God's Son who came to earth to pay the penalty of death for all those who believe on His Name.**

2. **Mankind is a natural born sinner who cannot enter the kingdom of God unless this sin has been washed away by the shed blood of Jesus Christ.**

3. **Jesus Christ is the one and only way to eternal salvation. There is no other way.**

4. **One must be truly "born again" in order to enter the kingdom of God. These are those who repent of their sins and render obedience by walking in the truths of God.**

5. **No one born of God makes a practice of sinning for God abides in him and he in God.**

6. **Jesus Christ is truly divine and existed from all eternity as the Son of God. He is the Word of God that was present when creation was spoken into being.**

7. **God speaks to His people in this life through both the Old & New Testaments. The Bible is God's revelation of Who He Is and Who We Are together with the relationship that exists between God and man. The Scriptures are not man's witness that God exists, but God's witness to man. The Bible was written by men who have been chosen by God. However, these men are not the authors of the bible – God is the true author for he breathes His words into the hearts of His chosen writers. Thus, the words in the bible are true in every respect.**

They will also warn mankind not to bow down and worship the Antichrist, and to not take the "mark of the beast." For those who take the "mark" will not enter into the Kingdom of God.

Notes:

(Slides # 35 - 36)

THE COMPLETION OF THEIR MINISTRY

The enemies of Christ will not be able to stop the two witnesses until the end of the 42 month period.

Key Points:

At that time, when their testimony is complete, the beast will be allowed to rise up against the two witnesses.

- The power of the Antichrist may not be fully manifested until the message of the gospel has been preached among all the nations and the testimony against the wicked world and against the false church has been finished.
- The world must hear the gospel message proclaimed by the true church and must hear it repeatedly, so they become fully conscious of their sin and the redemptive work of Jesus Christ.
- Those who reject Him will do so willingly and deliberately.
- Then the testimony is finished and may be silenced.

At this point the Antichrist will overcome the witnesses and kill them, but there will still be a remnant of saints who are alive at the second coming of Christ.

- Then the Antichrist will reign supreme and the world will rejoice and send gifts to one another, only because the church which spoke of blood and judgment has finally been overpowered; **or so they believe**.

This is the complete fulfillment of the following warning by Jesus to His disciples:

"If the world hates you, know that it has hated me before it hated you. If you were of the world, the world would love you as its own; but because you are not of the world, but I chose you out of the world, therefore the world hates you. Remember the word that I said to you: 'A servant is not greater than his master.' If they persecuted me, they will also persecute you. If they kept my word, they will also keep yours. But all these things they will do to you on account of my name, because they do not know him who sent me. ***John 15:18-21***

Notes:

____

____

____

BREAK-TIME (Slides # 37 - 38)

(Slide # 39)

A SECOND DEATH FOLLOWED BY A SECOND RESURRECTION

These witnesses will have completed their worldwide testimony after 42 months during which many among the world's population will have experienced tremendous "spiritual" revival.

Key Points:

- The earthly ministry of Jesus Christ is almost complete; there remains one more event that will be even more glorious than all which preceded it;
- An event which will bring finality to the Gospel of the Kingdom to the world.
- **That is the resurrection of the Body of Christ.**

Jesus' 1st, physical resurrection two-thousand years ago initiated a worldwide ministry that has resulted in millions of people entering into eternal life as sons and daughters of God.

- Now this 2nd, spiritual resurrection, through His Body of 144,000, will complete His ministry in this age.

Notes:

____

____

____

____

____

____

(Slides # 40 - 41)

A SECOND DEATH FOLLOWED BY A SECOND RESURRECTION

And when they have finished their testimony, the beast that rises from the bottomless pit will make war on them and conquer them and kill them, and their dead bodies will lie in the street of the great city that symbolically is called Sodom and Egypt, where their Lord was crucified. ***Revelation 11:7-8***

Key Points:

Here we see the first mention of the Antichrist who, at this point in time, is the ruler of the kingdom of the world. (Apollyon?)

- He is leading the charge to trample the blood of Christ under foot. Prior to the completion of their 42 month ministry, the world was not allowed to hinder them.[32]

- Just as the veil of protection was removed from Jesus Christ following His 3 ½ year ministry, it is also being removed from His Body of 144,000 chosen prophets following their 3 ½ year ministry.

- Now they are to be slain in view of the entire world in the streets of "the great city that symbolically is called Sodom and Egypt where their Lord was crucified."[33]

Is this "great city" literal Jerusalem?

- Some commentators say that it is symbolic of all cities worldwide who are immoral and rebellious against God (Sodom), who enslave God's people (Egypt), and who continually trample the blood of Jesus underfoot (where the Lord was crucified). Thus, they believe that these end-times witnesses are killed in cities throughout the world.

Perhaps this scenario is true but, also consider the following possibility.

- Recall that Jesus voluntarily went to Jerusalem knowing that it was time to lay down His life. Likewise, it is possible that the 144,000 will also be called by the Lord to travel to Jerusalem knowing that they too, are about to lay down their lives.

- It may be at a time when the Antichrist sets up the "abomination of desolation" on the temple mount and demands that the entire world bow down and worship it.

- Perhaps these 144,000 remnants of true Christianity will also ascend to the temple mount in Jerusalem and refuse to worship this image of the Antichrist.

- Subsequently, they will be beaten and killed with the entire world watching and cheering and celebrating by giving gifts to one another. Like a 4th of July party, they will probably set off fireworks around the world celebrating their supposed victory over the Kingdom of God.

Notes:

---

[32] Revelation 11:5
[33] Revelation 11:8

(Slides # 42 - 43)

A SECOND DEATH FOLLOWED BY A SECOND RESURRECTION

However, this is not the end of the ministry of these witnesses; for after 3 1/2 days the entire world will witness the resurrection of this great and numerous Body of Christ and watch in horror as they ascend to heaven.

But after the three and a half days a breath of life from God entered them, and they stood up on their feet, and great fear fell on those who saw them. Then they heard a loud voice from heaven saying to them, "Come up here!" And they went up to heaven in a cloud, and their enemies watched them. And at that hour there was a great earthquake, and a tenth of the city fell. Seven thousand people were killed in the earthquake, and the rest were terrified and gave glory to the God of heaven. ***Revelation 11:11-13***

A great earthquake rocks the city of Jerusalem killing 7,000 people. This will result in tremendous worldwide fear and perhaps many, like the Roman soldiers who crucified Jesus, will finally have their eyes opened and will give glory to God and to His Son. **Hopefully, these are people who have not yet taken the "mark of the Beast."**

- This is the second resurrection and will certainly cause more people among the nations to finally have their eyes opened to the truth of the atoning blood of Jesus and repent and begin to seek the Lord with their whole heart.

This would appear to be the last opportunity for mankind to respond to the gospel of Jesus Christ and enter into the Kingdom of God.

Notes:

(Slides # 44 - 45)

THE 7TH TRUMPET SOUNDS

Revelation 11:15-19

The message of the gospel of Jesus Christ to the world is now complete.

- The building of the spiritual temple is perfectly complete.

Now, the seventh trumpet sounds:

- The entire kingdom of heaven is now celebrating, but upon the earth, the greatest of all judgments are about to descent.

- Seven "bowls of wrath" are to be poured out across the entire earth.

Yet, more specifics are provided in Revelation 12 -14 which precede these seven "bowls of wrath."

- After which, the Lord Jesus will descend upon the earth with His mighty army.

- Then the dead will be raised for judgment. Then His sons and daughters will receive their great rewards earned during their lives upon the earth.

Notes:

____

____

____

____

____

____

Now remember, these sessions are taught chapter by chapter, but these chapters are not always chronological. <u>For example</u>:

- For example when this 7th trumpet is blown, it launches the seven bowls of wrath. **<u>Yet, we don't see the bowls poured out until chapter 16.</u>**

- Events concerning the gospel message of the two witnesses plus events in chapters 12 -14 also precede the seven bowls of wrath.

- Chapters 12 – 14 are designed to provide more insights into spiritual warfare and the reign of the Antichrist.

(Slide # 46)

THE NEXT SESSION:

First Read: Revelation 12

SPIRITUAL WARFARE BETWEEN THE WOMAN & THE DRAGON

- The Identity of the Woman
- The Dragon
- The Birth of the Male Child
- The War in Heaven
- The War Between the Woman & the Dragon
- Battlefield Tactics Employed by Satan
- Satan's Mission & Tactics for the End-Times
- Satan's Primary Objective in his War on Mankind

Additional Notes:

THE LAMB OF GOD - OUR TRUE "COMMANDER-IN-CHIEF"

The days are rapidly approaching when a tremendous separation will take place among mankind.

Yet, during this present era of warfare, He reigns as our Commander-in-Chief and His Name continues to be the battle cry for those warriors who fight daily for righteousness and truth.

His name is Jesus, Our Lord, Our King, Our Commander-in-Chief

- **A truly mighty Leader who would never delegate assignments to His people that He Himself wouldn't readily embrace.**

- **A Commander that Christian warriors will readily follow not matter the danger or what costs have to be paid.**

- **These are warriors whose deepest desire is to hear Jesus welcome them with the following words when they enter into His presence:**

> **......... 'Well done, good and faithful servant. You have been faithful over a little; I will set you over much. Enter into the joy of your master.'** ***Matthew 25:21***

THE LAMB OF GOD - OUR TRUE "COMMANDER-IN-CHIEF"

The days are rapidly approaching when a tremendous separation will take place among mankind.

Yet, during this present era of warfare, He reigns as our Commander-in-Chief and His Name continues to be the battle cry for those warriors who fight daily for righteousness and truth.

His name is Jesus, Our Lord, Our King, Our Commander-in-Chief

- **A truly mighty Leader who would never delegate assignments to His people that He Himself wouldn't readily embrace.**
- **A Commander that Christian warriors will readily follow not matter the danger or what costs have to be paid.**
- **These are warriors whose deepest desire is to hear Jesus welcome them with the following words when they enter into His presence:**

> **......... 'Well done, good and faithful servant. You have been faithful over a little; I will set you over much. Enter into the joy of your master.'** ***Matthew 25:21***

SPIRITUAL WARFARE
Between
THE WOMAN & THE DRAGON

(Revelation 12)

SESSION #8 – WORKBOOK
Intended For
"KINGDOM WARRIORS IN THE ARMY OF GOD"

Unveiling Mysteries in the "Book of Revelation"

Based upon the Book:

GOD'S ANOINTED WARRIORS

By

Dr. Donald Bell

Major USMC, Ret.

(Slides # 3 - 4)

THE WOMAN

And a great sign appeared in heaven: a woman clothed with the sun, with the moon under her feet, and on her head a crown of twelve stars. She was pregnant and was crying out in birth pains and the agony of giving birth. ***Revelation 12:1-2***

Key Points:

The woman appears so mighty and glorious that the sun, moon, and stars of heaven, all serve as signs to bring out the beauty and the authority that she has been given from on high.

Although she is currently suffering in her pregnancy, she is of tremendous importance to the Lord and His Kingdom.

(Slide # 5)

THE IDENTITY OF THE WOMAN

Listen to the Lord speaking to Satan after he enticed the fall of Adam and Eve into sin:

I will put enmity between you and the woman, and between your offspring and her offspring;
He shall bruise your head, and you shall bruise his heel." ***Genesis 3:15***

Key Points:

This verse is commonly referred to as the first covenant promise that our God made with mankind

Here the Lord is promising three things:

1. Satan and the woman were going to be enemies to each other.
2. Satan's descendants and the woman's descendants will be enemies to each other.
3. One of the woman's descendants would arise to bruise the head of Satan even though His heel would be bruised in the battle.

Notes:

____

____

____

(Slide # 6)

THE COMMISSION OF THE WOMAN

After speaking to Satan, the Lord tells the woman:

To the woman he said, "I will surely multiply your pain in childbearing; in pain you shall bring forth children. ***Genesis 3:16***

Key Points:

Her commission is two-fold – together with the Holy Spirit, she has been anointed to:

1. Give birth to the Messiah, the Son of God, who will destroy the effects of sin on mankind.
2. Give birth to all those of mankind who will eternally inhabit the Kingdom of God.

Thus, this woman is the symbolic mother of the people of God;

- She can be identified with true Israel in the old dispensation.
- She can be identified with the true Christian church in the new.

She is the Bride of Christ.

Notice that this woman, in all her glory, is also in a state of tremendous suffering supported only by the hope of a male offspring that she painfully awaits.

- According to various Old Testament scriptures, the heavy afflictions upon Israel that preceded the birth of the Savior are represented by these severe birth-pains.[34]

Suddenly, she sees a terrifying dragon, ready to devour her child as soon as HE is born.

Notes:

____

____

____

____

____

____

[34] Jeremiah 4:31; Micah 4:8-9

(Slides # 7 - 8)

THE DRAGON

And another sign appeared in heaven: behold, a great red dragon, with seven heads and ten horns, and on his heads seven diadems. His tail swept down a third of the stars of heaven and cast them to the earth. And the dragon stood before the woman who was about to give birth, so that when she bore her child he might devour it. ***Revelation 12:3-4***

Key Points:

- The dragon's kingdom is very powerful, as described by his appearance of seven heads, ten horns, and the seven crowns upon each of the heads.
- He also has a powerful demonic army as indicated by the "Stars cast down to earth." **Note**: At times, scripture uses "stars" to symbolize angelic beings.[35] In this case, they symbolize demonic angelic beings.

The seven heads are representative of all the evil empires that Satan uses throughout the centuries in his attempt to annihilate the Kingdom of God from the world. They are the:

- Egyptian Empire / Assyrian Empire / Babylonian Empire / Persian Empire / Greek Empire / Roman Empire / and the coming New World Empire.

Throughout the 4,000 years of the old dispensation, from the fall of mankind until the birth of Christ, Satan had been totally committed to identifying and annihilating all offspring originating from this woman, who was commissioned to give birth to the Kingdom of God upon the earth.

He was especially focused on the promised One who God said would have the power to crush him and destroy his plans for the world.

Notes:

[35] Revelation 1:20

(Slide # 9)

SATAN'S TACTICS TO DEFEAT THE BIRTH OF THE MALE CHILD

Key Points:

Note his Old Testament tactics:

1. **Initially, he probably believed that Abel was the chosen one and so, he had Cain murder him.** *But then Seth was born and the spiritual seed of the woman begins to multiply through the line of Seth.*

2. **In Genesis 6, we learn that he got the "sons of God", who were angelic beings, to marry the natural "daughters of men" in order to merge together the human and demonic angelic race and thus eliminate the possibility of a righteous seed arising from a woman.**[36] *Again, God counterattacks this tactic through the Great Flood, and saves the seed of the woman through the family of Noah.*

After the flood he changed his tactics:

3. First, he attempted to control the population of the entire world at the tower of Babel. When that failed:
4. He attempted to enslave the nation of Israel in Egypt. When that failed:
5. He attempted to annihilate them as a nation using the Assyrians, the Babylonians, and the Persians.
6. When Satan saw that he couldn't completely annihilate them, he attempted to rule over them through the mighty Grecian and Roman empires.

Throughout this entire 4,000 year period Satan was intent on either preventing the birth or murdering the child, yet he did not know who HE would be or when HE would be delivered by the woman.

Notes:

[36] Genesis 6:1-4; Jude 1:6-7

(Slide # 10)

THE BIRTH OF THE MALE CHILD

She gave birth to a male child, one who is to rule all the nations with a rod of iron, but her child was caught up to God and to his throne, ***Revelation 12:5***

Key Points:

- The time finally arrived when the woman, through the Holy Spirit of God, gave birth to the Savior that had been promised some 4,000 years earlier.

- Satan didn't know who the natural mother would be, but he did know through earlier prophecies that the birth would be in the town of Bethlehem.

Suddenly, the angels of heaven loudly proclaimed the glory of the birth of Christ. [37]

- Now Satan learns who He is and immediately, he enticed the Judean king Herod, a servant of the dragon, to take whatever measures were necessary to have this newborn child slain.

- Herod then dispatches soldiers to Bethlehem who murdered all the children under two years of age that he might make sure of destroying the one hated Child.[38]

But in spite of all this, the Promised One appears, Christ is born.

- Now, the dragon was not certain how Christ intends to gain the victory over him although now, he recognizes Him as the Promised One whom the Lord said would "crush his head."

Notes:

BREAK-TIME (Slides # 11 - 12)

[37] Luke 2:14

[38] Matthew 2:16-18

(Slides # 13 thru 19)

SATAN'S TACTICS TO DEFEAT THE MISSION OF JESUS

Key Points:

1. **Satan employs two different tactics to usurp the mission of God for His Son, Jesus:**

- First, Satan attempts to subject Him spiritually as he offers Jesus the kingdoms of the world if He would only bow down and worship him.[39]
- When this fails he arouses the religious leaders of the day, to continually come against Him throughout His 3 ½ year ministry.

2. **Yet, a time had been ordained from the beginning when Jesus was to be cutoff after 3 ½ years of ministry** and thus, His enemies were allowed by God to seize Him; whereupon they vented all their anger and jealousy by severely mocking and beating Him.

- Eventually they crucified Him in the midst of two thieves intending to display Him as simply another criminal in Israel.
- **(Note: Read Psalm 22:11-18 and listen to what was in the heart of Jesus as He suffered on the cross).**
- Now Satan thought that he had "crushed the head" of God's chosen King and thus, turned the tables on God's promise to crush his head.

3. **What he didn't realize was that the victory for the people of God's Kingdom lay in the way of the sacrifice of the perfect Lamb of God.**

- For sin is what gives the devil his claim for the possession of mankind and now sin itself has been cast out of those of mankind who will embrace the sacrificial Lamb that the Lord Himself has provided.

4. **THE DECEIVER HIMSELF HAS BEEN DECEIVED!**

Notes:

[39] Matthew 4:1-11

(Slide # 20)

SATAN'S ACCESS TO THE THRONE ROOM OF HEAVEN

Key Points:

The scriptures of the Old Testament clearly reveal that Satan had access to the courts of heaven and could stand in the presence of Almighty God.[40]

- Historically, Christ had not yet "crushed the head" of the serpent and thus, had not yet assumed dominion over the citizens of the Kingdom of God.
- Satan was still the sovereign ruler of this world and he argued that all of mankind came under his dominion due to their sin which disallowed them access before the presence of Almighty God.[41]
- Jesus Himself referred to Satan as "The Ruler of this World."[42] He is also referred to as the "Prince of the power of the air who is the spirit that is working in the sons of disobedience.[43]

However, the counsel of our Lord countered Satan's argument.

- That eternal counsel of our Lord established that not only the Christians who are born on earth following the sacrifice of Christ are His chosen people, but it pertained also to those who had been born before the crucifixion. (Abraham, Moses, David, etc)

Note: The parable of Lazarus & the rich man who died and went to Hades where they saw Abraham. [44]
Also Note: When Jesus died, He descended into hell where he freed those in captivity who then ascended to the presence of the Father. (Some were also seen in the streets of Jerusalem) [45]

Notes:

____

____

____

(Slide # 21)

THE WAR IN HEAVEN

(Revelation 12: 7-9)

Now war arose in heaven, Michael and his angels fighting against the dragon. And the dragon and his angels fought back, but he was defeated and there was no longer any place for them in heaven. And the great dragon was thrown down, that ancient serpent, who is called the devil and Satan, the deceiver of the whole world— he was thrown down to the earth, and his angels were thrown down with him. ***Revelation 12:7-9***

[40] Job 1:6; 2:1; Zechariah 3:1
[41] John 14:30; Ephesians 2:1-3
[42] John 12:31; 14:30
[43] Ephesians 2:2
[44] Luke 16:19-31
[45] Matthew 27:51-53

Key Points:

Now, the head of the Lord's army was Michael, an angelic general:

- Michael appears in scripture to be in command of the entire angelic army that is assigned to protect God's chosen people during their life on earth,

- Also, Michael confronts the claims of Satan for the souls of the Old Testament saints.[46]

Satan is about to reap what he has sown as Michael and his angelic army are about to throw him and his demonic army out from the heavens and the presence of the Lord, and down to earth.

Notes:

(Slide # 22)

THE WAR IN HEAVEN

(Revelation 12: 10-12)

Finally, when Christ comes, suffers, pays the death penalty for the sins of His people, and ascends to heaven to sit at the right hand of Almighty God, the battle is finally decided in favor of Michael and his army of angels.

A great voice sings out:

"Now the salvation and the power and the kingdom of our God and the authority of his Christ have come, for the accuser of our brothers has been thrown down, who accuses them day and night before our God. And they have conquered him by the blood of the Lamb and by the word of their testimony, for they loved not their lives even unto death. Therefore, rejoice, O heavens and you who dwell in them!
But woe to you, O earth and sea, for the devil has come down to you in great wrath, because he knows that his time is short!" ***Revelation 12:10-12***

[46] Jude 9; Matthew 24:31; Luke 4: 10-11; Daniel 12:1

Key Points:

This is the death blow to Satan; it was probably shouted by Michael and his angelic army at Satan and his demonic army in a power so great that this mighty enemy was finally cast out of heaven.

- Satan has lost the battle in the heavenlies, but he will never surrender; he must be completely defeated.
- Now that he has been cast down to earth, his wrath is directed toward the woman and her offspring, who remain upon the earth; and the conflict continues to this present day.

Notes:

BREAK-TIME **(Slides # 23 - 24)**

(Slide # 25)

THE WAR BETWEEN THE WOMAN & THE DRAGON

(Revelation 12: 6 & 13-17)

Now the scene shifts back to the earth where the woman continues to bring forth offspring.

> And when the dragon saw that he had been thrown down to the earth, he pursued the woman who had given birth to the male child. ***Revelation 12:13***

Key Points:

- Satan failed to prevent the birth of Christ, and he failed in his centuries-long war with Michael; and now, being filled with a raging fury, he is intent on pursuing and wiping out Christianity from the face of the earth.
- His initial tactic is one of murderous persecution of those who truly profess Jesus as their Lord. These are the citizens of the Kingdom of God who continue to oppose Satan and his purposes among mankind and therefore, he is committed to annihilating true Christianity from the face of the earth.
- Many Christians in the early church were brutally martyred by governments and religious groups under the influence of Satan. However, Christianity (represented by the "woman") continued to grow in the midst of persecution.
- Satan pursued the woman, but the Lord intervened and enabled the woman, with two wings of the great eagle, to fly into the wilderness where Satan could not go.

The remainder of this chapter is a prophetic picture of all that has and will take place throughout the Christian era.

Notes:

(Slides # 26 thru 28)

THE WILDERNESS

But the woman was given the two wings of the great eagle so that she might fly from the serpent into the wilderness, to the place where she is to be nourished for a time, and times, and half a time. **Revelation 12:14**

- Satan pursued the woman, but the Lord intervened and enabled the woman, with two wings of the great eagle, to fly into the wilderness where Satan could not go.

Key Points:

Now, where is this wilderness?

- It is the Kingdom of God in the midst of the world.
- Read John 17:14-18 where Jesus is Praying to His Father for the protection of His People.

This wilderness is representative of that spiritual place in the midst of the world where God's people are nourished from on high and where neither Satan nor his legions can enter.

- It is that place where the Lord reigns in the hearts of His people. Although it lies right in the midst of the world, yet it is separated from the world.[47]
- It is that place where the people of God who reside in the world are spiritually separated from the worldly lifestyle for those in the wilderness live by the principles of God.
- This wilderness, which is the invisible Kingdom of God, exists throughout the world among every nation.

Notes:

[47] John 15;19; 17:16

(Slide # 29)

SATAN'S WARFARE AGAINST THOSE IN THE WILDERNESS

Although Satan cannot pursue the woman into the wilderness, he can certainly employ military tactics against her with the mission of destroying her or rendering her impotent on the battlefield.

Key Points:

- His initial tactic in the first centuries of Christianity was one of persecuting Christians using segments of the Roman government.
- It was Satan's plan to murder the leaders of the early Christian movement and to create fear of persecution among the masses but, it backfired on him.
- Great numbers of Christians were martyred, yet the gospel continued to go forth on the soaring strength of "eagle wings" and this period of intense martyrdom by secular government against the righteous only resulted in the Kingdom of God growing greater and stronger than ever before.
- As long as the Christian church remained in a state of separation from the world, the armies of Satan were impotent against it.

Notes:

____

____

____

____

____

(Slides # 30 - 31)

SATAN'S WARFARE AGAINST THOSE IN THE WILDERNESS

The serpent poured water like a river out of his mouth after the woman, to sweep her away with a flood. But the earth came to the help of the woman, and the earth opened its mouth and swallowed the river that the dragon had poured from his mouth. ***Revelation 12:15-16***

He opens his mouth and casts a huge stream of water in to the wilderness designed to wash the church out of the wilderness and unite it with the world.

- This stream of water is symbolic of deceptive lies from the mouth of Satan.

Key Points:

Now, the wilderness is also a place where the hearts of professing believers are "tested."

- Those who truly remain steadfast in their faith are protected from this flood of the Serpent and are led by our Lord Jesus through the wilderness journey of this life.
- However, like the exodus wilderness in the days of Moses, there is a large segment of Christianity who would rather enjoy the comforts of the world rather than the hardships of the wilderness; which is designed to prepare His people for entry into the Promised Land.

Therefore, a large segment of the church that initially entered the wilderness is now brought out on the flood waters of Satan.

- These are a people who profess faith in Christ, but actually worship the things of the world.
- They voluntarily choose to leave the wilderness for they want to enjoy the worldly comforts of this life while still believing that they belong to the Lord.
- What they fail to realize is that the wilderness is where God dwells in the midst of His people and they have departed from His presence.

They are used by Satan to establish religious organizations to mock the theology and persecute those who remain faithful in the wilderness.

- This began with the formation of the Roman Catholic Church and continues to this day. The Catholic Church is very much of the world. Her popes have built an unrivaled worldwide empire of property, wealth, and influence.
- Claiming to be the bride of Christ, the Roman Catholic Church has been in bed with godless rulers throughout eighteen centuries of history.

Notes:

(Slide # 32)

AMERICA – INITIALLY A CHOSEN WILDERNESS

When the fires of religious persecution waxed hotter and hotter over the European continent, the Lord again provided a refuge where His people might be nourished from the face of the serpent in the "wilderness" of the Western Hemisphere.

Key Points:

- He supplied them with "eagle's wings" to the land of America where they were delivered out of the abyss of Roman Catholicism and where Protestantism was allowed to grow.[48]

Immediately thereafter, Christian missionaries were dispatched to take the gospel of Christ to foreign nations all around the globe.

- Thus, over the last three hundred years, Christianity grew stronger and stronger around the world as Christians in the midst of this western wilderness proclaimed the gospel protected from the persecution of the enemy.

(Slide # 33 - 34)

SATAN'S WARFARE TACTICS - A FLOOD OF FALSE DOCTRINES

The serpent poured water like a river out of his mouth after the woman, to sweep her away with a flood. **Revelation 12:15**

Here Satan is forced to change tactics when he fails to merge all the Christian institutions with the world; he now turns to individual believers.

- He does this by "mouthing" a flood of false doctrines and heresies throughout the Christian and governmental institutions in both Europe and America.[49]

Key Points:

Such is the present method of satanic attack in the west as lies from the mouth of Satan have become popular teachings not only in our country's school system, but in many false churches that claim to embrace Christian doctrines.

[48] Philip Mauro, *Things Which Soon Must Come to Pass* (Reiner Publications, Swengel, PA, 1974) p.384-389
[49] Herman Hoeksema, *Behold, He Cometh* (Grand Rapids, MI: Reformed Free Publishing Assn, 1969) p.448-449

For example, Satan, appearing as an "angel of light", has convinced the majority of American institutions that:

- Jesus Christ is not really the Son of God, but merely a good man who sets a fine example for us to follow.
- Man is basically righteous and we must stop listening to those who proclaim that all are born sinners.
- God is really not our Creator, but we are merely a product of evolution.
- The bible was written by ancient men as they perceived the world of their day and although it contains many good lessons for us, it really is not the "Word of God."
- Whether we are evangelical Christians, Catholics, Muslims, Buddhists, or Hindus; we all serve the same god.
- Eventually all persons will have eternal life and we will all become like god.

Notes:

(Slides # 35 - 36)

GOD INTERVENES & SATAN IS ENRAGED

Although many of the "seed" sown on rocky ground or among thorns embrace these deceptive lies, the true people of God who are the "seed" sown in fertile soil are those who remain in the wilderness and have been protected by our Lord from this "flood of lies."

But the earth came to the help of the woman, and the earth opened its mouth and swallowed the river that the dragon had poured from his mouth. **Revelation 12:16**

When this tactic failed to deceive those who remained steadfast in the Kingdom of God, Satan became enraged and is now totally committed to gathering all the worldly forces to wipe out true Christianity, together with the nation of Israel, from the face of the earth.

Key Points:

The lies of Satan are currently being heard and received among those who place their hope in a world and are looking to establish a one world government without God. They are intended:

- To convince the great majority of the world that proclaiming Jesus Christ as the only way to eternal life is detrimental to society and should be outlawed.
- The elimination of both Jews and uncompromising Christians would certainly be helpful to the establishment of worldwide peace.

I truly believe that we are now in the generation of mankind when Satan is preparing his military forces to completely erase the name of Jesus Christ from the face of the earth.

> Then the dragon became furious with the woman and went off to make war on the rest of her offspring, on those who keep the commandments of God and hold to the testimony of Jesus. And he stood on the sand of the sea. **Revelation 12:17**

As he stands on the "sand of the sea" - He is about to call up his son (Antichrist) to rule over the entire world.

Notes:

BREAK-TIME **(Slides # 37 - 38)**

(Slide # 39)

NOURISHED IN THE WILDERNESS FOR 3 ½ YEARS

It is also said that the woman will be nourished for 3 ½ years in the wilderness.

Then the woman fled into the wilderness, where she has a place prepared by God, in which she is to be nourished for 1,260 days. **Revelation 12:6**

Key Points:

- Although the woman has been pursued throughout the Christian era - this 3 ½ years of living in the wilderness appears to be that final period of time when the Christian church witnesses under the protection of the Lord during the first 3 ½ year reign of the Antichrist.
- It is a time when a powerful and glorious anointing is on the sealed 144,000 as they proclaim the gospel truths in great power throughout the world.
- They are protected from the Antichrist and his legions during this time.

Additionally, this period of 3 ½ years is certainly meant to encourage those in the Kingdom of God that our wilderness journey will one day come to an end.

- Then comes the time to enter into our real home, the eternal Promised Land.

Notes:

(Slide # 40)

REVIEWING SATAN'S WARFARE OBJECTIVES

The mission which drives his evil heart may be summarized as follows:

Satan's Mission Statement
"To ascend into the heavens where I will raise my throne above the stars of God and make myself like the Most High where I will continue to challenge His sovereign rulership over all of creation".[50]

He knows that if he can prevent all of mankind from professing loyalty to the Almighty Father and His Son; then Satan himself would become the recipient of all worship and glory throughout the earth.

He also intends to show the entire angelic realm that he is a leader to be worshipped and will prove it by controlling those of the Lord's creation who were created in "His image."

Key Points:

The principal tactic used to accomplish this was and still is; deception.

- He deceives mankind into believing that the tremendous potential that resides within us can be more fully realized by living life under our own guidance rather than under God's.
- Thus, he convinces the majority of mankind that they have no need for God and that; they could be their own gods doing whatever is pleasing to them, even if it is harmful to others. This self-centered nature is really the nature of Satan.

Secondly, he intends to rid the world of all those who are not deceived and are totally committed to God the Father and to His Son, Jesus Christ.

- He does this by convincing world governments, together with false religions, that God's people are the only obstacle that keeps them from achieving their worldly goals and so, they must be either converted to the world's belief system or be killed.
- If Satan can defeat the Army of God on earth, then he will certainly claim that God's Word concerning earthly redemption has been voided by the powers of darkness and that he alone is worthy to rule over all of creation.

Thus, his commitment to destroy God's beloved witnesses from the face of the earth is tremendously strong.

[50] Isaiah 14:12-14

(Slide # 41)

SUMMARY OF REVELATION 12

Two thousand years are compressed into a few verses in this chapter of Revelation. The intent was to reveal the purposes of Satan as well as the protection and purposes of God with respect to the war between the kingdoms.

Key Points:

- This brings us up to the time when the final battle will be fought, but this battle will be greater and more powerful than any previous event in history.
- One last supreme effort awaits release of a powerful gospel to peoples of all nations. This will be a gospel released through the Body of Christ; and His 144,000 witnesses for 3 ½ years throughout the days of Great Tribulation.
- These are those who "keep the commandments of God and hold to the testimony of Jesus" right up to that day of their martyrdom.

The next session presents an overview of this final battle and the tactics soon to be used by Satan and his dark forces in both the human and spiritual realms.

(Slide # 42)

THE NEXT SESSION:

First Read: Revelation 13

THREE BEASTS – AN UNHOLY TRINITY

➢ A Beast Rises Up from the Sea.	Seven Heads of the Beast.
➢ Antichrist – A Final World Ruler.	Antichrist – The Appearance of Invincibility.
➢ Antichrist – His Popularity & #666.	The Coming of the Two-Horned Beast.
➢ The False Prophet – His 3-Fold Ministry.	A Seven Year Covenant.
➢ Purpose for the Tribulation.	Purpose for God's Wrath.

➢ **Our Lord's Calling – "Endure & Remain Faithful"**

THE LAMB OF GOD - OUR TRUE "COMMANDER-IN-CHIEF"

The days are rapidly approaching when a tremendous separation will take place among mankind.

Yet, during this present era of warfare, He reigns as our Commander-in-Chief and His Name continues to be the battle cry for those warriors who fight daily for righteousness and truth.

His name is Jesus, Our Lord, Our King, Our Commander-in-Chief

- **A truly mighty Leader who would never delegate assignments to His people that He Himself wouldn't readily embrace.**

- **A Commander that Christian warriors will readily follow not matter the danger or what costs have to be paid.**

- **These are warriors whose deepest desire is to hear Jesus welcome them with the following words when they enter into His presence:**

> **......... 'Well done, good and faithful servant. You have been faithful over a little; I will set you over much. Enter into the joy of your master.'** ***Matthew 25:21***

THREE BEASTS

------ ------ ------

AN UNHOLY TRINITY

(Revelation 13)

SESSION #9 – WORKBOOK

Intended For

"KINGDOM WARRIORS IN THE ARMY OF GOD"

Unveiling Mysteries in the "Book of Revelation"

Based upon the Book:

GOD'S ANOINTED WARRIORS

By

Dr. Donald Bell

Major USMC, Ret.

(Slides # 2 thru 4)

THREE BEASTS – AN UNHOLY TRINITY

The purpose of this session is to prepare soldiers in the army of God by providing advance intelligence concerning the dark and terrifying leadership that will soon arise from among the nations of the world.

- This will be a time of great trouble as evil leaders, who have been anointed by Satan, will be obsessed with eliminating the kingdom of God from the face of the earth and establishing an antichristian power throughout the earth.

Key Points:

If Satan is to successfully complete his mission of worldwide conquest, he must quickly rally the entire world to unite under his lordship.

- So far he has been unable to destroy the woman in the wilderness, but he has developed a terrible new plan.
- He is about to establish the greatest and most powerful kingdom in the age of mankind.
- A kingdom that will be led by two men anointed with monumental satanic power.
- Their primary mission is to rally the entire world to rise up and devour all those who faithfully proclaim the name of God the Father and His Son, Jesus Christ.

Thus, this phase of John's vision begins with Satan, the dragon, standing alongside the sea, knowing that his time is rapidly running out.

Notes:

(Slide # 5)

A BEAST RISES UP FROM THE SEA

And I saw a beast rising out of the sea, with ten horns and seven heads, with ten diadems on its horns and blasphemous names on its heads. ***Revelation 13:1***

- John is a witness to this yet future event when he sees a dreadful beast possessing tremendous power rising up out of the sea.

Key Points:

The sea is frequently symbolic in Scripture of agitated and troubled peoples and nations who are controlled by the power of sin.

For example:

- *But the wicked are like the tossing sea; for it cannot be quiet, and its waters toss up mire and dirt.* ***Isaiah 57:20***
- *And the angel said to me, "The waters that you saw, where the prostitute is seated, are peoples and multitudes and nations and languages.* ***Revelation 17:15***

Therefore, this beast arises from the midst of tumultuous nations who have been experiencing tremendous devastations and are crying out for a Hollywood-type savior.

- It is quite probable that this troublesome period on the earth is the aftermath of the "trumpet series" of events; a time of famine, plagues, and a terrified populace caused by events that wiped out 1/3 of mankind and the natural resources of the earth.

Notes:

(Slide # 6)

A BEAST RISES UP FROM THE SEA

In the previous chapter, Satan, the Dragon, was symbolized by seven "crowned heads" along with ten horns.[51]

- Here in this chapter, the Beast from the sea is described as having **seven heads and ten "crowned horns."**

Key Points:

Thus, this Beast from the sea is not Satan, but it resembles him, and is submissive to Satan's authority.

- The Dragon is the most ferocious of all beasts and here we see that he intends to give his power and authority to his "beastly son" (the Antichrist), who will use it in an attempt to carry out his father's purposes.
- Satan is a spirit and as such, he cannot establish an earthly throne in person. He needs a human agent to be subject to him as a world ruler.
- Thus, the Antichrist is about to receive what Jesus Christ refused when Satan offered Him all the kingdoms of the world in exchange for His allegiance.[52]

Notes:

[51] Revelation 12:3

[52] Matthew 4:8-10

(Slide # 7)

A BEAST RISES UP FROM THE SEA

Beasts in scripture are frequently symbolic of great world empires.[53] These empires all have different characteristics even as wild beasts are different.

- They may differ in strength, courage, speed, viciousness, and crushing power much like leopards, bears, and lions differ from one another. Some are nobler than others and some are more despicable.

Key Points:

This final beast combines all the characteristics of the great empires which have historically ruled parts of the world.

- This terrible Beast arising out of the sea is symbolic of that last evil kingdom that will reign during the time known as the Great Tribulation.
- It will have the courage and ferocity of a lion, will conquer with the speed of a leopard, and possess the merciless crushing power of a bear.
- This final world power does not consist of just one nation and one people; but it combines within itself all the evil character and powers of every worldly kingdom that has historically arisen in opposition to the Kingdom of God.

Notes:

[53] Daniel 7-8

SEVEN HEADS OF THE BEAST

And I saw a beast rising out of the sea, with ten horns and seven heads, with ten diadems on its horns and blasphemous names on its heads. And the beast that I saw was like a **leopard**; its feet were like a **bear's**, and its mouth was like a **lion's** mouth. And to it the dragon gave his power and his throne and great authority. ***Revelation 13:1-2***

Key Points:

The seven heads are representative of great empires that have historically risen to oppose the Kingdom of God throughout the centuries.

At the time that John received this vision, around 95AD, he was told that five of these empires had already fallen; one was currently ruling; and the last one was yet to come.[54]

- The "five" that had already fallen were the **Egyptian** Empire, the **Assyrian** Empire, the **Babylonian** Empire, the **Persian** Empire, and the **Grecian** Empire. (These last three were symbolized by a lion, bear, and leopard in Daniel's vision).
- The sixth empire that was currently ruling during John's vision was the **Roman** Empire.
- Although these six historical empires have all been great and powerful, none has ever succeeded in attaining universal power over the entire earth, nor have they been able to overcome the Kingdom of God.

Notes:

[54] Revelation 17:9-10

(Slide # 10)

SEVEN HEADS & TEN HORNS OF THE BEAST

Key Points:

Unlike the first six kingdoms, the last kingdom will come by a confederation of prominent nations rather than by military conquest.

- This is represented by the "ten horns" which is symbolic of a final manifestation of United Nations which will all be of one mind.

Satan has learned that one nation cannot accomplish world domination.

- It needs to be a league formed of the "seventh head" made up of the "ten horns" who will eventually give their power over to a man.[55]
- This is the Beast in its entirety; a confederation of world powers being of one mind and giving all of their power over to a man. This is also the resurrection of the old kingdom of Nimrod's Babel, a united confederation, in modern form.[56]

The seventh head of this beast, together with the ten horns, represents the "end times" kingdom which collides with Jesus Christ and His mighty army in the final conflict preceding His second coming.

Notes:

BREAK-TIME (Slides # 11 - 12)

[55] Revelation 17:11; Daniel 7:8

[56] Herman Hoeksema, *Behold, He Cometh* (Grand Rapids, MI: Reformed Free Publishing Association, 1969), p.576

(Slides # 13 - 14)

ANTICHRIST – THE FINAL WORLD RULER

Key Points:

From within this seventh kingdom will arise a leader who will personify the darkness of Satan in the flesh; an "anointed one" whom Satan has chosen to rule over this final demonic kingdom.

- This is the Antichrist, Satan's messiah to the world, who possesses his father's image and will require all the earth to bow down and worship his spiritual father.
- Just as Jesus is the Son of God who came in the flesh to redeem His people out of the world, now the Antichrist is the son of Satan who comes in the flesh to eliminate the people of God from the face of the earth.
- The Antichrist will honor all who acknowledge him and set them up as rulers and reward them with land and wealth taken from among the people. [57]

Because of the apparent relationship of the ten horns to the Roman Empire revealed in the book of Daniel, it appears as if the Antichrist may arise out of a modern culture that is descended from the ancient Roman Empire.[58]

- However, he may or may not presently be a citizen of any contemporary European, Middle Eastern, or northern African nations who were once a part of the Roman Empire.
- It's possible that he could even be an American whose ancestors came from a region that was once under the control of the Roman Empire.

Notes:

---

[57] Daniel 11:39

[58] Daniel 7:8

(Slides # 15 - 16)

ANTICHRIST – HIS POPULARITY

Key Points:

The Antichrist will emerge on the world's political scene in the aftermath of worldwide economic, environmental, and military disasters.

- He gains control by stepping up at this time and mesmerizing the masses into believing that he alone is the one who can lead the world into peace and prosperity through a multitude of promised "changes."
- He will seduce many with flatteries to the point where even the wise among the people will stumble and be led astray.[59]
- He probably is quite handsome and certainly has a charismatic personality that can mesmerize the masses like a popular rock music celebrity.
- All they know is when they see and hear this man speak, it makes them feel "warm and fuzzy" inside. They relish the vague terms of "hope" and "change." He will be perceived by the masses as their true savior.

Although the man known as the Antichrist will be charismatic, he will also be very firm in his speech and probably with eyes that appear hypnotic, along the lines of Adolph Hitler's.

- Being possessed by Satan, he will have the fierce countenance of a lion; flattering, but very dangerous to those who will not idolize him.

Notes:

[59] Daniel 11:32; 35

(Slides # 17 - 18)

ANTICHRIST – THE APPEARANCE OF INVINCIBILITY

One of its heads seemed to have a mortal wound, but its mortal wound was healed, and the whole earth marveled as they followed the beast. And they worshiped the dragon, for he had given his authority to the beast, and they worshiped the beast, saying, "Who is like the beast, and who can fight against it?" ***Revelation 13:3-4***

Key Points:

Somewhere in his rise to absolute power, he receives a mortal wound to the head that appears to be fatal. This will probably occur when his popularity is growing for it appears as if the entire world is aware of this apparently fatal incident.

- Perhaps he will physically suffer an assassination attempt which is falsely published in the media as having been fatal.
- Suddenly he will "miraculously" recover, and the world will marvel as if their heroic messiah has been raised from the dead.
- This wound may be faked, or it may be real but nevertheless, this perceived resurrection will result in much loyalty from the world.

This supposed death of Antichrist and his miraculous recovery is intended to paint a parallel picture with the death of Christ and His resurrection.

- This tactic of the Dragon is designed to weaken the gospel message that the death and the resurrection of Jesus Christ is the only path to eternal life.

Finally, he will certainly convince the world that he is invincible when he brings down three powerful nations in his rise to power.[60] Perhaps the assassination attempt will emanate from among these three nations. At any rate, the world will shout:

"Who is like the beast, and who can fight against it?"[61]

Notes:

---

[60] Daniel 7:7-8

[61] Revelation 13:4

(Slides # 19 thru 22)

THE COMING OF THE TWO-HORNED BEAST

(Revelation 13:11-17)

There is a second agent through whom Satan will use to war against the Kingdom of God.

> Then I saw another beast rising out of the earth. It had two horns like a lamb and it spoke like a dragon. It exercises all the authority of the first beast in its presence, and makes the earth and its inhabitants worship the first beast, whose mortal wound was healed. ***Revelation 13:11-12***

Key Points:

He is commonly referred to as the False Prophet.

- He will personify the tenderness and love of a lamb, yet it will be a deceptive form of love, for he will soothingly preach comfort-sounding lies intended to gain the loyalty of mankind through trickery.

The primary mission of the False Prophet will be to bring all of mankind to worship the Antichrist.

- He will have supernatural skills of persuasion as he promotes the Antichrist as a great man with a tremendous love for his people and who will bring peace and prosperity to the world.
- The False Prophet is the workhorse who causes the people to turn to Antichrist. Both are used to delude the masses and exercise their authority over the world.
- Antichrist represents the Kingdom of the World in the political and military realms while the False Prophet deals with the religious, moral, and commercial aspects of this society.

Together with Satan, the Antichrist and the False Prophet will constitute an unholy trinity of malicious evil.

- As Christ received authority from His Father, so Antichrist receives authority from the Dragon; and as the Holy Spirit glorifies Christ, so the False Prophet glorifies the Antichrist.

Notes:

____

____

____

____

____

____

BREAK-TIME **(Slides # 23 – 24)**

THE FALSE PROPHET – HIS THREE-FOLD MINISTRY

1 - Signs and Wonders:

It performs great signs, even making fire come down from heaven to earth in front of people, ***Revelation 13:13***

Key Points:

He will publicly perform incredible signs and wonders before the world for the purpose of demonstrating his supernatural authority.

- This will cause the world to embrace him as a true prophet to whom they must show great respect and obey his every command.
- These miracle workings of the False Prophet will also persuade the vast majority of peoples that the god of the False Prophet is greater than all other gods.

The result of these "showy miracles" will surely shift the focus of many away from the works of Christian disciples to the person of the Antichrist.

- He intends to undermine the works and miracles of the disciples of Jesus Christ who will also be sharing the gospel together with miraculous works during this period of time.

The healing and other miracles of our Lord through the work of His disciples will be directed to needy individuals from a pure heart of love.

- This is in opposition to the miracles of the False Prophet who performs them before the world solely for the purpose of demonstrating supernatural power.
- Those who experience the miracles of God in their life will probably not be deceived by the False Prophet and therefore, the Kingdom of God will continue to increase.

The sincere love emanating from Christ's warrior army for the common people will be clearly obvious to many when compared to Satan's disciples who will resemble popular performing stars designed to enamor the masses.

Notes:

(Slides # 27 thru 30)

THE FALSE PROPHET – HIS THREE-FOLD MINISTRY

2 - Erect an Image of Antichrist:

………and by the signs that it is allowed to work in the presence of the beast it deceives those who dwell on earth, telling them to make an image for the beast that was wounded by the sword and yet lived. And it was allowed to give breath to the image of the beast, so that the image of the beast might even speak and might cause those who would not worship the image of the beast to be slain. ***Revelation 13:14-15***

Key Points:

The False Prophet will command the people to make an "image of the Antichrist" which will then be given breath to speak.

- When this image is complete, all the inhabitants of the world will be required to worship it.
- Those who refuse to worship this "speaking image" will be sought out and slain.

This "image" is somewhat difficult to envision. Let's look at a couple of possible scenarios:

Perhaps this may resemble a "golden image" like that erected by Nebuchadnezzar in ancient Babylon who required all persons to bow down and worship it or be put to death.[62]

- Only this image is in the likeness of the Antichrist. However, if this image of Antichrist is located in a particular geographic area, then it would require television type technology to visibly manifest it around the world.
- If so, there would probably be a law requiring all to gather before a picture of this image and worship it at designated times throughout their daily routine.

A second scenario could be that a new religious organization would be setup using existing church facilities around the world where people would gather and worship the Antichrist.

- This religious organization would then be the "speaking image."
- Envision this in a nation of Christianity: statues and pictures of Christ, together with any sign of a cross would all be replaced with this image of the Antichrist.
- All peoples would then be required to join and regularly worship in these churches.

Notes:

[62] Daniel 3:1-7

(Slides # 31 thru 33)

THE FALSE PROPHET – HIS THREE-FOLD MINISTRY

3 - Mark of the Beast = 666:

Also it causes all, both small and great, both rich and poor, both free and slave, to be marked on the right hand or the forehead, so that no one can buy or sell unless he has the mark, that is, the name of the beast or the number of its name. This calls for wisdom: let the one who has understanding calculate the number of the beast, for it is the number of a man, **and his number is 666.** ***Revelation 13:16-18***

The False Prophet will command that mankind must receive the mark of the beast in order to participate in the marketplace.

Key Points:

The mark is the number of a man and this number is 666.

The mark not only identifies those who worship the Antichrist, but it appears as if this number will one day identify the man himself.

Numbers are also used to provide deeper understanding of certain passages in scripture. In this passage, the number "6" is commonly understood to represent man, while the number "3" is representative of our Triune God.

- Therefore, 666 is man attempting to be god, but will never reach the number "7" which represents perfection.
- However, I wouldn't recommend that we spend time attempting to satisfy our curiosity by attempting to identify potential antichrists.
- It will be plain to the people of God when he arrives on the world scene as the sole leader.

The primary purpose for the mark is to control all of the world's commercial activity. In order to legally buy or sell in this anti-Christian kingdom, one must have this mark upon the forehead or the right hand.

Notes:

(Slide # 34)

THE FALSE PROPHET – HIS THREE-FOLD MINISTRY

3 - Mark of the Beast = 666:

Key Points:

Who are those who receive the mark on their forehead, and who are the ones who receive it on their right hand?

- The forehead is the most exposed and conspicuous part of the body. Perhaps this will be reserved for the leaders in commerce and government so that they may be immediately recognized.
- If so, the mark on the right hand is for the common workers who are also committed to the Antichrist.

This mark will also be beneficial for those among the Body of Christ since its absence, provides a visible means of identifying those who remain faithful to the Lord.

- The ongoing gospel message being proclaimed during this period will most certainly include warnings against receiving this mark of the beast. [63]
- Many will fall away, yet many will remain faithful unto death.
- They may not be able to buy or sell, but they will faithfully cling to the name of Jesus.

Thus, in the midst of tribulation, God's mighty warriors will be social outcasts in the world, but will maintain. <u>"The Lord Almighty is our God, and Christ alone is our King". And they will not be ashamed.</u>

[63] Revelation 14:9-10

Notes:

(Slides # 35 – 36)

SATAN'S TACTICS MANIFESTED IN THE HEADS OF THE BEAST

Satan has historically employed two primary tactics in his zealous rage to obliterate the Kingdom of God from the earth:

Key Points:

First:

- **He uses an all-out frontal assault with the intent of completely annihilating the world of Christianity from the face of the earth.**

This has been historically manifested time and again as God's people have been frequently in danger of complete annihilation. Following is a brief examination of Satan's tactics using the first six heads of the beast in their warfare against the Kingdom of God.

We can expect to see these same tactics being used in the future.

- Brutal enslavement: can expect mass imprisonment in concentration camps.
- Women and children being targeted for slaughter in order to create tremendous fear among the masses. This is certainly a favorite tactic among the cowardly Islamic terrorists.
- Murder of the elderly and newborn babies for purpose of controlling population growth.
- Brutal and humiliating torture. For example: The Assyrians captured many Israeli army leaders who were lifted naked, but alive on the heads of spears and paraded them in front of their families & fellow countrymen.
- Destruction of all Christian bibles, music, and worship under the threat of death. Antiochus Epiphanes of the Grecian Empire outlawed the worship of the God of Israel and declared that all Hebrew Scriptures were to be destroyed.

Notes:

____

____

____

____

____

____

____

____

(Slides # 37 thru 39)

SATAN'S TACTICS MANIFESTED IN THE HEADS OF THE BEAST

Key Points:

Second:

- **To entice God's people to voluntarily turn from the worship of the Lord to worshipping the "prince of this world."**
- This is the more preferable tactic of Satan since he takes much greater pleasure in turning a man's heart than in killing him. He believes that this proves that he is more worthy of worship than the Lord.

Some historical examples:

1. **Enticed the Israeli's with the Egyptian lifestyle.**

- Instead of trusting the Lord during the hardships encountered in the wilderness, they grumbled and wanted to return to Egypt.
- This may parallel a great falling away during tribulation times.
- This will be manifested at "decision-time" when all are required to take the "mark of the beast."

2. **The influences of the Greek culture which encouraged self-seeking pleasures and immorality.**

- Many of the Israeli youth of that day scorned the traditions of Israel, undid their circumcision, and embraced the immoral pleasures of the Greeks.
- This is very prevalent in today's western culture which emphasizes commercialism, sexual immorality, and entertainment as the epitome of an enviable lifestyle.

3. **The Roman Empire established a powerful and dark authority within Christianity that was designed to turn Christian worship away from Christ and to human representatives – popes and saints.**

- Today's false Christian churches will support this antichristian kingdom and will be a major player in the betrayal of true believers who refuse to compromise their faith.

Christian soldiers, we must anticipate that similar tactics will be employed by the enemy with even greater power in the seventh kingdom ruled by the Antichrist.

Notes:

____

____

____

(Slide # 40)

A SEVEN YEAR COVENANT

Key Points:

As we've seen in a prior session, Jesus Christ comes to confirm the true covenant between God, His Father, and all who embrace Him as their Lord. It is a covenant which ushers in everlasting righteousness and ends with the anointing of a most holy place.[64]

However, there is also a covenant that will soon be established by Satan, who is intent on counterfeiting the true works of Jesus Christ.

- This covenant, or peace treaty, is made by Israel without the Lord and is described in Scripture as the "covenant with death" because it is made with the sons of darkness, and will be confirmed by the Antichrist.[65]
- However, after 3 ½ years this dark covenant which was founded on lies will be broken by the Antichrist, who will then set up his own image in the Jerusalem temple.
- The setting up of this satanic image in a newly built temple in Jerusalem will be the sign of the beginning of that Great Tribulation which will suddenly ensnare the world.[66]

Jesus confirms His Father's covenant when He kept the law perfectly and then laying down His life at the cross for the sins of mankind.

- Thus, after 3 ½ years, Jesus Christ gave His own life as a perfect sacrifice and thereby, did away with the need for the sacrificial system of the Old Covenant.[67]
- Antichrist appears to be counterfeiting the 3½ year ministry of Christ by his first 3½ years of uniting world governments.

[64] Daniel 9:24
[65] Daniel 9:27; 11:22-24; Isaiah 28:15-22
[66] Matthew 24:15-22
[67] Hebrews 10:8-10

Notes:

BREAK-TIME (Slides # 41 – 42)

(Slide # 43)

THE PURPOSE FOR THE "TRIBULATION"

Key Points:

What is "tribulation?"

- Tribulation is a time of warfare between the forces of good and evil.
- It is an attack of the world's system against the true believers of Jesus Christ.

Good and evil cannot coexist. The characteristics of each become more prevalent during a time of conflict.

- As the battle intensifies, the peoples among both sides become more visible and neutrality begins to disappear. Weeds among the church are continually exposed as they fall away and side with the religiosity of the world.
- The armies of the world become larger and darker and more violent in their hatred against God and His people.
- At the same time, the Army of God becomes stronger and more radiant as they stand for the truth of God and His Spirit grows stronger and stronger among them.

Tribulation will increase in escalating stages, yet so will the strengthening of His army.

- This tribulation pressure takes place because of God's love for mankind and His desire to bring out of darkness unto salvation every single soul possible and to destroy every demonic stronghold that has held the human race captive.
- Lukewarm Christianity will collapse during the Great Tribulation.

Notes:

(Slide # 44)

THE PURPOSE FOR THE "WRATH OF GOD"

Key Points:

The Wrath of God is a military action on the part of the armies of heaven to avenge and rescue God's people in the world.

- It is manifested primarily in the "opening of the seven seals," the "blowing of the seven trumpets," and the "pouring out of the seven bowls of wrath."
- God's wrath is directed solely against the forces of darkness.
- However, there are currently many in the world of darkness that will be called into the light.
- Many warnings are poured out from heaven that tend to either draw people to the Lord or to solidify their hatred toward Him. [68]
- What restrains the outpouring of God's wrath is the ability of His people to maintain their stand and communicate their faith.
- When this is complete and God's message is shut down within His people, then the full wrath of God will be poured out on the earth.

Notes:

[68] Dan Juster and Keith Intrater, *Israel, the Church and the Last Days* (Destiny Image Publishers, 1991), p. 137-147

(Slide # 45)

OUR LORD'S CALLING: "ENDURE & REMAIN FAITHFUL"

If anyone is to be taken captive, to captivity he goes; if anyone is to be slain with the sword, with the sword must he be slain. **Here is a call for the endurance and faith of the saints**. ***Revelation 13:10***

Key Points:

Antichrist is not looking solely for political control of the world; he is intent on receiving worship from every single individual that lives on earth.

- The working of miracles and the requiring of image worship, together with a marked body, are all designed to visibly identify and unite the individual peoples among the nations in loyalty to Antichrist as well as to one another.
- They are also intended to help identify those persons who will refuse to receive the mark of the Antichrist or bow down to his image.
- These faithful believers will be classified as enemies among the nations and a hindrance to world peace.

Notes:

(Slides # 46 – 47)

OUR LORD'S CALLING: "ENDURE & REMAIN FAITHFUL"

Key Points:

The world system shall make war against the people of God who continue to witness during the reign of this Antichrist.

- These are warriors who refuse to submit to his authority, and maintain that it is not Antichrist, but Christ who is their King.
- They will be deeply hated, and the world will wage a continuous war against them and eventually overcome them.

- These will be extremely hard and faith challenging days; days of persecution and a time of "wearing out" the people of God.
- All bibles and other biblical books will be outlawed, and the peoples will be required to turn them over to the authorities for burning. Those who refuse will be criminally charged and sentenced to imprisonment.
- Murderous executions, imprisonment in concentration camps, brutal torture, causing separation from family, not allowing food and water to be purchased will all be commonly employed tactics of this evil kingdom. **These are the days of persecution.**

Notes:

____

____

____

(Slide # 48)

IMPRISONMENT VERSUS EXECUTION

Key Points:

One may wonder why imprisonment of many of God's people is employed by the enemy instead of simply executing them.

- Imprisonment allows time for the enemy to break down the spirit of people for the purpose of allowing them to voluntarily turn away from the Lord and render allegiance to the Antichrist.
- Satan rejoices when men visibly turn away from Almighty God and render allegiance to him, even if it is not from a pure heart.

- Turning men onto him is more important than murdering them since he has defeated what is most important to God; that being, the steadfast faithfulness of His people.

- The one who has turned away from the Lord will be undoubtedly praised before the world as a newly enlightened hero. **<u>This will be a shameful experience</u>**.

Notes:

(Slide # 49)

WHERE IS OUR "HIDING PLACE?"

<u>Key Points:</u>

Our Lord will provide a hiding place for us when the time of persecution arrives. Where is that hiding place?

- For the prophet Daniel, it was both in a king's palace and in a lion's den.
- For Shadrach, Meshach, and Abednego, it was in a fiery furnace.
- For Joseph, it was in an Egyptian prison.
- For David, it was in a cave out in the wilderness.
- For the apostle Paul, it was in prison or shipwrecked in the Mediterranean.
- For the spies sent by Joshua, it was in a harlot's house in Jericho.
- For Corrie Ten Boom, it was in a flea-infested barracks in a Nazi concentration camp.

They were all right where God wanted them and not a hair on their head perished. So our hiding place is wherever the center of the Lord's will is for us. The only thing we should fear is being out of God's will.

- Trust in the Lord for our individual hiding places for they will probably be different for every believer in the End Times.
- Meanwhile stand in the gap and prepare our brothers and sisters for the coming hour of trial.

Notes:

(Slides # 50 - 52)

REJOICING IN THE MIDST OF PERSECUTION

Key Points:

Although Christians will be physically overcome during this horrendous period of time; they are the ones who are victorious in this war.

- They will become outcasts from society, mocked at by former neighbors, family members, and friends; perhaps imprisoned and killed.
- This is the Body of Christ having a similar experience that their Lord Jesus Christ endured 2,000 years earlier. They are now glorious participants in His great victory.
- In the crucial test of faith, they have chosen to relinquish their lives rather than their faith in their God. This is true victory.

"Blessed are those who are persecuted for righteousness' sake, for theirs is the kingdom of heaven." Blessed are you when others revile you and persecute you and utter all kinds of evil against you falsely on my account. Rejoice and be glad, for your reward is great in heaven, for so they persecuted the prophets who were before you. ***Matthew 5:10-12***

Count it all joy, my brothers, when you meet trials of various kinds, for you know that the testing of your faith produces steadfastness. And let steadfastness have its full effect, that you may be perfect and complete, lacking in nothing. ***James 1:2-4***

In this you rejoice, though now for a little while, if necessary, you have been grieved by various trials, so that the tested genuineness of your faith—more precious than gold that perishes though it is tested by fire—may be found to result in praise and glory and honor at the revelation of Jesus Christ. Though you have not seen him, you love him. Though you do not now see him, you believe in him and rejoice with joy that is inexpressible and filled with glory, obtaining the outcome of your faith, the salvation of your souls. ***1 Peter 1:6-9***

Notes:

____

____

(Slides # 53 thru 57)

A CHINESE SONG – "TO BE A MARTYR FOR THE LORD"

Many attend that big American church and hear that if you serve God, you will be healthy and prosperous. In China, it's the exact opposite. You may be healthy and prosperous before you are a Christian, but once you start serving God, seldom will you stay that way.

- Chinese Christians have learned to be committed in their faithfulness even though they realize that they may be torn from their families and martyred.

The following song has been very popular in the Chinese underground churches: [69]

From the time the early church appeared on the day of Pentecost,
The followers of the Lord all willingly sacrificed themselves.
Tens of thousands have sacrificed their lives that the gospel might prosper.
As such they have obtained the crown of life.
Those apostles who loved the Lord to the end
Willingly followed the Lord down the path of suffering.
John was exiled to the lonely isle of Patmos.
Stephen was crushed to death with stones by the crowd.
Matthew was cut to death in Persia by the people.
Mark died as his two legs were pulled apart by horses.
Doctor Luke was cruelly hanged.
Peter, Philip, and Simon were crucified on the cross.
Bartholomew was skinned alive by the heathen.
Thomas died in India as five horses pulled apart his body.
The apostle James was beheaded by King Herod.
Little James was cut up by a sharp saw.
James the brother of the Lord was stoned to death.
Judas was bound to a pillar and died by arrows.
Matthias had his head cut off in Jerusalem.
Paul was a martyr under Emperor Nero.

I am willing to take up the cross and go forward,
To follow the apostles down the road of sacrifice.
That tens of thousands of precious souls can be saved,
I am willing to leave all and be a martyr for the Lord.

To be a martyr for the Lord,
To be a martyr for the Lord,
I am willing to die gloriously for the Lord.

---

[69] Randy Alcorn, *Safely Home*, (Carol Stream: Tyndale House Publishers, Inc., 2001) p.288-289

(Slide # 58)

THE NEXT SESSION:

First Read: Revelation 17 - 18

Mystery Babylon –
The Capital of Wealth, Pleasure, & Harlotry

- Identifying the City of Mystery Babylon.
- The Woman who Rides the Beast.
- Who is this Woman?
- What is her Relationship to the Beast?
- The Woman Loves the Beast – The Beast Hates the Woman.
- Her great fall – She will burn in a day.
- The Parallelism between the United States and Mystery Babylon.
- Our Lord's Calling – "Come Out of Her, My People."

Additional Notes:

THE LAMB OF GOD - OUR TRUE "COMMANDER-IN-CHIEF"

The days are rapidly approaching when a tremendous separation will take place among mankind.

Yet, during this present era of warfare, He reigns as our Commander-in-Chief and His Name continues to be the battle cry for those warriors who fight daily for righteousness and truth.

His name is Jesus, Our Lord, Our King, Our Commander-in-Chief

- **A truly mighty Leader who would never delegate assignments to His people that He Himself wouldn't readily embrace.**
- **A Commander that Christian warriors will readily follow not matter the danger or what costs have to be paid.**
- **These are warriors whose deepest desire is to hear Jesus welcome them with the following words when they enter into His presence:**

.... 'Well done, good and faithful servant. You have been faithful over a little; I will set you over much. Enter into the joy of your master.' ***Matthew 25:21***

MYSTERY BABYLON

-------- -------- --------

THE CAPITAL OF POWER, WEALTH, & IDOLATRY

(Revelation 17 - 18)

SESSION #10 – WORKBOOK
Intended For
"KINGDOM WARRIORS IN THE ARMY OF GOD"

Unveiling Mysteries in the "Book of Revelation"

Based upon the Book:

GOD'S ANOINTED WARRIORS

By

Dr. Donald Bell
Major USMC, Ret.

(Slides # 4 thru 7)

A PROSTITUTE RIDES THE BEAST

Then one of the seven angels who had the seven bowls came and said to me, "Come, I will show you the judgment of the great prostitute who is seated on many waters, with whom the kings of the earth have committed sexual immorality, and with the wine of whose sexual immorality the dwellers on earth have become drunk." And he carried me away in the Spirit into a wilderness, and I saw a woman sitting on a scarlet beast that was full of blasphemous names, and it had seven heads and ten horns. ***Revelation 17:1-3***

And on her forehead was written a name of **mystery**: "Babylon the great, mother of prostitutes and of earth's abominations." ***Revelation 17:5***

Key Points:

Now who this ungodly woman is, what she represents, and where she exists today is extremely important to God's mighty warriors of this generation:

- Concerning her identity, many have struggled with the fact that Mystery Babylon is pictured as both a woman and a city seated on many waters.
- However, in order for God's chosen people in our generation to refuse to have fellowship with her, they must be able to discern who or what she is during these times.
- She is capable of such great deception that everyone who follows her will eternally be lost. Unfortunately, many who attend today's Christian churches have fallen in love with her.

Listen to our Lord who commands us to:

.........Come out of her, my people, lest you take part in her sins, lest you share in her plagues; for her sins are heaped high as heaven, and God has remembered her iniquities." ***Revelation 18:4-5***

Then He goes on to say:

For this reason her plagues will come in a single day, death and mourning and famine, and she will be burned up with fire; for mighty is the Lord God who has judged her." ***Revelation 18:8***

This is so very important for our comprehension as most teachers of Revelation simply warn Christians about receiving the "mark of the Beast."

- **Yet, Mystery Babylon will be burned up prior to the supreme reign of the Antichrist as evidenced by the 10 kings who will not receive their royal power in a one world government until she is destroyed.**

(Slide # 8 - 9)

MYSTERY BABYLON PRECEDES THE ANTICHRIST

Key Points:

The Book of Revelation is not necessarily chronological. Frequently, a general vision is first recorded and then later visions are given to provide additional detail. For example:

- The events recorded in chapters 17 & 18 concerning Mystery Babylon and the seven-headed beast **actually occur prior to the reign of the Antichrist** recorded in chapter 13.

For here we see in chapter 17, as the harlot woman continues to ride the beast, the ten kings have not yet received their royal power.

And the ten horns that you saw are ten kings who have not yet received royal power, but they are to receive authority as kings for one hour, together with the beast. ***Revelation 17:12***

Yet, when Antichrist first appears in chapter 13, these 10 kings have received their royal power.

This is apparent by the crowns on the heads of the ten kings in chapter 13.

And I saw a beast coming out of the sea. He had ten horns and seven heads, with ten crowns on his horns, and on each head a blasphemous name. ***Revelation 13:1(NIV)***

- **These ten crowns are symbolic of "royal power" given to these kings.**

They have as king over them the angel of the bottomless pit. ***Revelation 9:11***

And as previously addressed in a session #6 – this is most likely - the Antichrist.

However, here in Revelation 17, we see that the beast has not yet risen, but is about to arise from the bottomless pit.

The beast that you saw was, and is not, and is about to rise from the bottomless pit and go to destruction. ***Revelation 17:8***

As you examine both of these verses - it appears to indicate that the Antichrist arises out of the devastation known as the "trumpet series" that destroyed 1/3 of the entire earth – and it is also very probable that this trumpet series of events will result in the destruction of that harlot woman, known as Mystery Babylon.

Key Points:

In fact, the one-world government which will be ruled by the Antichrist will only come to "ultimate power" after the destruction of Mystery Babylon. At that time, these 10 kings will receive their royal authority.

- One needs to understand who, what, and where she currently resides in the today's world if they plan to survive her destruction for she will be "burned up" in a single day.

Perhaps "Mystery Babylon" is the primary target in the "trumpet series" which destroys 1/3 of the earth. This is speculative but very probable.

Notes:

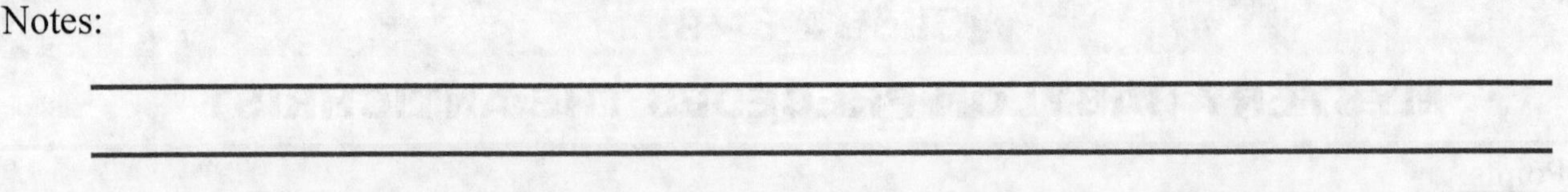

(Slides # 10 - 11)

HISTORICAL ATTEMPTS TO IDENTIFY MYSTERY BABYLON

John sees this harlot woman sitting on the beast that has seven heads and ten horns. These seven heads are described as seven mountains, and also, as seven kings.

This calls for a mind with wisdom: the seven heads are seven mountains on which the woman is seated; they are also seven kings, five of whom have fallen, one is, the other has not yet come, and when he does come he must remain only a little while. ***Revelation 17:9-10***

Key Points:

Our early Christian fathers who experienced the horrendous evils of Roman Catholicism through the dark ages strongly believed that John was seeing a vision of the power of the Roman papacy represented by this harlot woman seated on seven mountains.

- Claiming to be the bride of Christ, the Roman Catholic Church has been in bed with godless rulers down throughout NT history. She has partied with these kings and made both them and their respective nations drunk with the wine of her spiritual fornications.[70]
- Her cup is also filled with the blood of saints, for she has been responsible for the murder of millions of the Lord's sons and daughters through the centuries.
- Because of her worldwide influence and wealth, every world leader will have to deal with the Roman Catholic Church in order to attain and maintain political power.
- Therefore many renowned theologians believed that these mountains are representative of the city of Rome which is known for being built upon seven hills.

However, mountains in scripture are also frequently symbolic of mighty empires.[71]

- Just as a mountain is visibly manifested high above the normal surface of the earth, these ancient empires were the greatest among all the surrounding nations in the world.
- Thus, it is probable that this mysterious Babylonian woman, who rides on the top of these symbolic mountains, is the primary controlling influence over all the great empires that have arisen over the centuries.

Remarkably, she is astride the seven-headed beast which apparently reveals that she is the one that steers the direction of the mighty kingdoms of the World. Five of these heads are representative of great empires that existed prior to the Roman Empire.

[70] Dave Hunt, *A Woman Rides the Beast*, (Eugene: Harvest House Publishers, 1994) p. 70-71
[71] Jeremiah 51:25; Daniel 2:35; Zechariah 4:7

(Slide # 12)

BABYLON THE GREAT– A CONTROLLING INFLUENCE OVER MIGHTY NATIONS

Those familiar with the Book of Daniel will remember the man-like statue in Nebuchadnezzar's dream which portrayed the different parts of the human body as representative of mighty world empires?

- These were empires which would arise and oppress the people of God prior to both the first and the second coming of the Lord Jesus Christ.[72]

Key Points:

Recall that the "head of gold" was representative of the Babylonian empire.

- Now we always recognize a person by looking at their face, which provides the identity for the entire body. The head consists of the eyes, the ears, and the brains; all of which develop the vision and guide the rest of the body in the direction the head desires to go.
- Therefore, the successive kingdoms that have risen to power after the fall of the Babylonian Empire are all part of this Mystery Babylon. They are intent of ridding the world of God's chosen people.
- Babylon is the "head" that controls the affairs of the world and the authority that oppresses the people of God throughout all the ages since the beginning of time.
- These kingdoms first arose in the Middle East where they all warred against the nation of Israel but over the last 2,000 years, during the era of Christianity, she has slowly moved westward.

Notes:

[72] Daniel 2

(Slides # 13 - 15)

MYSTERY BABYLON – A "GREAT CITY"

This evil woman is also referred to five different times as representative of the "great city."
For example:

And the woman that you saw is the great city that has dominion over the kings of the earth." ***Revelation 17:18***

Note the following parallel with another woman who is also symbolic of a great city:

The New Jerusalem
Then came one of the seven angels who had the seven bowls full of the seven last plagues and spoke to me, saying, "Come, I will show you the Bride, the wife of the Lamb." And he carried me away in the Spirit to a great, high mountain, and showed me the holy city Jerusalem coming down out of heaven from God, having the glory of God, its radiance like a most rare jewel, like a jasper, clear as crystal. ***Revelation 21:9-11***

Key Points:

These are two spiritual capital cities; The New Jerusalem represents the Kingdom of God and Mystery Babylon represents the Kingdom of the World.

- New Jerusalem is symbolic of the Bride of Christ and Mystery Babylon is symbolic of a prostitute.
- Now a prostitute is used in Scripture as one who claims to be a worshipper of God, but secretly, she whores with the world.
- These two cities also have physical locations. Babylon currently exists within the world while New Jerusalem resides in heaven awaiting its time to descend to the earth.

Now does the city commonly known as Mystery Babylon have a single geographical location? Well, yes and no!

- She is that city where the idolatry of commercialism, immorality, and hatred of God exists.
- **She is worldwide, yet she is located more strongly in certain sections of the world**.

Additionally, many believe that Mystery Babylon is representative of the world-cities of today; such as, New York, Paris, Chicago, Rome, London, Los Angeles, Hollywood, etc, etc.

- These are cities in supposedly Christian nations that have exported evil across the globe.
- Thus, they see her as the city-prostitute who commits fornication with all the nations of the earth and reigns from a city which is the center of world-wide commerce and industry.

However, can we really equate "Mystery Babylon" with any single city or geographical area? Perhaps!

Notes:

____

____

____

____

____

____

BREAK-TIME **(Slides # 16 - 17)**

(Slide # 18)

BABYLON THE GREAT – A UNITING OF POLITICS, COMMERCIALISM, & RELIGION

Every mighty world empire has embraced these three sources of power within society – politics, commercialism, and religion.

Key Points:

Now - note the ones who will mourn the destruction of the woman, Mystery Babylon:

1. The "Kings of the Earth" represent the political and military arena. (18:9)
2. The "Merchants of the Earth" represent the commercial arena. (18:11)
3. The "Unfaithful Woman" represents the idolatrous religious arena. (17:5-6)

The uniting of these three elements of society represents a gigantic system in pursuit of power and wealth; **but also promising the assurance of eternal security in the after-life**.

- The great majority of peoples want that assurance of a good life following their death – thus, over the centuries; various worldwide religions have grown rich, powerful, and controlling.

The focus of the citizens of Babylon is to achieve more and more earthly riches and comforts without the hand of God.

- Babylonian laws are continually passed to accommodate their worldly pursuits.

- These are laws contrary to the Laws of God for they are laws designed to appeal to mankind's desire to be their own gods and control their own destiny. Certainly sounds familiar in today's world.

Notes:

(Slides # 19 - 20)

THE HARLOT WOMAN & COMMERCIALISM

While commerce is a legitimate pursuit of profit, *Commercialism* is an attitude of the heart that can grow into the religion of Money worship.

- The great world of commercialism has become virtually a religion to countless millions of people; its leaders who are the captains of industry are practically the rulers of the world.

The world of commercialism is tangible and visible, but the animating spirit behind it all is that love of "Money."

- Money is the god that many worship in our day for a man's true god is that to which he consecrates his life. Money is the greatest of all the idols in our generation.

- **It is the greatest rival of God for the affections and devotions of man. Jesus warns us:**

"No one can serve two masters, for either he will hate the one and love the other, or he will be devoted to the one and despise the other. You cannot serve God and money. **Matthew 6:24**

Key Points:

The harlot woman appears to be in control of worldly governments because of her great riches and the millions who continually seek comfortable answers for their lives.

- These followers of the woman are in pursuit of worldly riches and comforts, but they are also seeking assurance that their happiness will continue in the eternal realm after their death.

- Thus, both "religion" for its millions of followers and "commercialism" for its wealth are extremely powerful and generally control the affairs of public life.

- Therefore, "politicians" have to climb into bed with this Great Babylonian Whore in order to gain the support of the majority of people.

All the injustices that are committed in the commercial and religious segments of society are symbolized by this harlot woman.

- Her cup is full of the abominations of an evil worldly kingdom that has persecuted the true people of God since the beginning of time.

Notes:

(Slide # 21)

THE HARLOT WOMAN & POLITICS

Key Points:

Her worldly views of politics embrace a leftist view of government - which emphasizes the rights of liberal-minded human beings - even at the expense of righteousness and justice.

- This is so prevalent today within those cities and states controlled by liberal minded, leftist politicians – who support the rioters taking over cities in our once beloved nation.

- Their acceptable philosophy is that all mankind is basically good - and any acts of evil are the result of living in a poor environment.

They encourage individual rights which approve of abortions, same-sex marriages, releasing of criminals on legal technicalities, etc.

- No matter what they say – these leftist governments do not care for those citizens that voted them into office – they simply want to control them while seeking for more and more power and riches.

Notes:

(Slide # 22)

THE HARLOT WOMAN & FAMILIES

Key Points:

If American family life would obstruct the development of their socialistic worldview; it also must be transformed.

- Child discipline is viewed as outdated and criminal. Divorce is acceptable in this society and adultery is certainly not frowned upon.
- If free love, homosexual marriages, and the murder of unborn children are advantageous to the establishment of a united worldly kingdom – its practice must be encouraged.

Notes:

(Slide # 23)

THE HARLOT WOMAN & SCHOOLS

Key Points:

Schools are also required to teach this socialistic worldview. They may not teach a definite religion, nor allow prayer - that would not be in harmony with a universal brotherhood.

- Differences of opinion must be removed - and an acceptable socialistic state of things must be established, taught, and accepted by the students.
- Youth education that supports same-sex marriages and homosexuality as a normal and acceptable lifestyle is becoming mandatory.
- The students who refuse to adhere to these socialistic beliefs will be mocked, ridiculed and labeled as religious fanatics.
- A time is coming when they may also be torn from their families - and forced to integrate into this leftist, socialistic environment.

Notes:

____

____

____

____

____

(Slide # 24)

THE HARLOT WOMAN & RELIGIOUS POWER

The followers of this harlot woman are in pursuit of worldly riches and comforts in this life BUT:

Key Points:

- They are also seeking assurance that their happiness will continue in the afterlife following their death.
- So churches are welcomed in the worldly society BUT the only acceptable gospel message must be a social gospel – that is, a gospel of love and peace for all mankind, BUT without Jesus Christ being involved.
- This social gospel will encourage their followers that they are not spiritually impotent, but that they are truly divine.
- That is, human beings are not natural sinners, but they are by nature – righteous children of God.

Both "religion" for its millions of followers seeking security in the afterlife and "commercialism" for its wealth are extremely powerful and generally control the affairs of worldly life.

Key Points:

- Politicians have to embrace this Great Babylonian harlot in order to gain the support of the majority of people, which will allow them to succeed in rulership over the various nations of the world.
- All the injustices that are committed in the social, commercial, and religious segments of society are symbolized by this harlot woman.
- Her cup is full of the abominations of an evil worldly kingdom - that has persecuted the true people of God since the beginning of time.
- **Whereas Jesus Christ, whose followers have no place in this world, -- has commanded His people to take the lowest place in it.**

Notes:

BREAK-TIME **(Slides # 25 - 26)**

(Slides # 27 thru 29)

Eight Steps to Breakdown Freedom & Establish Socialism

1. **Healthcare** – a nation that controls healthcare controls the population.
2. **Poverty** – Increase the poverty level and the poor people become much easier to control - and then they will embrace a government that promises to supply all of their needs.
3. **Debt** – Increase the debt to the point that you can increase the taxes, which will produce more poverty.
4. **Gun Control** – To remove the ability of people to defend themselves - which will allow the government to create a very nasty police state.
5. **Welfare** – Take control of every aspect of peoples lives. That is food, housing, income, etc. Go after those who are hoarding food and ammo.
6. **Education** – Take control of what people read and listen to - as well as taking control of what children learn in school. That is – control over both schools and media.
7. **Religion** – Remove the belief of God from both governmental institutions and the schools.
8. **Class Warfare** – Create division between the middle-class workers and the poor.

- This will cause great discontent that will make it easier to tax the middle class and promise more support to the non-working populace.
- However, the truly wealthy are the ones who support a socialistic state in order to control their nations.
- A socialistic state must do away with the middle class which will allow the wealthy to control all commerce.

Key Points:

This certainly sounds like the agenda of the leftists politicians in America.

- Saul Alinsky merely simplified the plan of Vladimir Lenin's scheme for world conquest by communism.

Even Stalin, that evil communist dictator back in the 40's and 50's - described his communist converts as "Useful Idiots."

- And look at how these "Useful Idiots" have destroyed every nation in which they have been used to seize power and control.
- And all this is presently happening at an alarming rate in the Divided States of America.

The leftist governors, city mayors, and congressmen in our nation certainly view these BLM rioters as "useful idiots."

- These are mindless, rioting mobs that have no idea that they are being used to destroy their own freedoms and create a dark, demonic, socialistic state which will eventually enslave them.

- This blindness that exists within these rioting mobs is such a shame – these are men and women who have no idea that they are being controlled by demonic leadership.

- As Christians we really need to show compassion, - not disgust, - and continually pray that many of them will wake up and rise up - out of this deep darkness and into the light - of the Lord's Kingdom.

Notes:

(Slides # 30 - 31)

THE BEAST = POLITICAL & MILITARY POWER

This seven headed beast that is being guided by the harlot woman represents the political and military powers of the world.

Key Points:

Remember that the six heads of the "beast" represent six stages of development of various kingdoms which existed in the past while the coming kingdom of the Antichrist is represented by the seventh head.

- While the ten horns represent ten powerful kings who will rule during the final manifestation of the seventh kingdom.
- This future realization of the seventh kingdom shall come into being by a united confederation of nations rather than by military conquest.
- They will unite and establish their final antichristian kingdom with the Antichrist as the supreme world ruler.

Thus, the seventh head is representative of a league of nations who will anoint the Antichrist as the ruling authority over the final world empire.

- They will be viciously dedicated to wiping out the people of Christ from the face of the earth which will provide more blood for their rich and beautiful whore.

These are the days that our Lord calls the "great tribulation."

For then there will be great tribulation, such as has not been from the beginning of the world until now, no, and never will be. And if those days had not been cut short, no human being would be saved. But for the sake of the elect those days will be cut short. ***Matthew 24:21-22***

Those who endure the great tribulations without compromise their faith will eventually receive tremendous glory as they stand in the presence of God the Father and His Son, Jesus Christ.

Notes:

(Slide # 32)

THE 8TH BEAST = THE WORLD RULER

Now there is an eighth beast that is distinct from the other seven:

As for the beast that was and is not, it is an eighth but it belongs to the seven, and it goes to destruction. And the ten horns that you saw are ten kings who have not yet received royal power, but they are to receive authority as kings for one hour, together with the beast. These are of one mind and hand over their power and authority to the beast.
They will make war on the Lamb, and the Lamb will conquer them, for he is Lord of lords and King of kings, and those with him are called and chosen and faithful." ***Revelation 17:11-14***

Key Points:

This is not simply another human ruler – this is the Antichrist.

- Daniel describes him as another horn among the ten with eyes like a man and a mouth speaking great things; even greater than his companions.
- He blasphemies Almighty God and makes war with the followers of Christ.
- Daniel also tells us that he overthrows three of the ten horns in his rise to supreme power.[73]
- This 8th beast is Satan manifested in human form. Antichrist – the messiah to the world.

However, before this eighth beast, the Antichrist, can come into supreme worldwide power, he must control all the commercialism and religions of the world.

- Thus, he must overthrow the woman who symbolizes that great and immoral city of Babylon.
- This overthrow of Mystery Babylon will take place in a single day without any advance warning.
- The world will be in tremendous shock and grief as their idols are suddenly swept away and are about to be replaced by a single man.

This will be a quick and powerful attack on the areas in which the harlot exercises the greatest control; a place where all the merchants of the earth were in bed with her.

Notes:

____

____

____

[73] Daniel 7:8; 20-22; 24-25

(Slides # 33 - 35)

THE WOMAN LOVES THE BEAST
BUT
THE BEAST HATES THE WOMAN

This harlot woman is committed to the beast for it is because of its political and military powers that she is enriched. However, unknown to this woman, the beast is not committed to her, but is using her to gain power in the world governments.

- The Antichrist will suddenly attain supreme power by burning this Mystery Babylon and taking control over all of her commercial and religious activities.

> And the ten horns that you saw, they and the beast will hate the prostitute. They will make her desolate and naked, and devour her flesh and burn her up with fire, for God has put it into their hearts to carry out his purpose by being of one mind and handing over their royal power to the beast, until the words of God are fulfilled. ***Revelation 17:16-17***

And:

> For this reason her plagues will come in a single day, death and mourning and famine, and she will be burned up with fire; for mighty is the Lord God who has judged her." ***Revelation 18:8***

This sudden attack appears to be nuclear for it is described as being a great fire with rising smoke that is seen from far off.

> For in a single hour all this wealth has been laid waste." And all **shipmasters** and seafaring men, sailors and all whose trade is on the sea, stood far off and cried out as they saw the smoke of her burning, "What city was like the great city?" ***Revelation 18:17-18***

Following the destruction of Mystery Babylon, the final kingdom will be committed to bring all sources of power under the complete control of the Antichrist:

Commercialism will continue to exist for those embracing the "mark of the beast."
- But, free enterprise among the merchants of the earth will disappear. "No one can buy or sell unless they have the mark of the beast!"
- This new world money system will be the lifeblood of the beast government of Antichrist.

Religion will continue to exist for those worshipping the "image of the beast."
- But, freedom to worship other gods will disappear.

Yet a remnant of God's chosen people previously identified as the 144,000, will not take the mark of the beast nor will they bow down to his image.

- **They will continue to be a strong and powerful light in the midst of this darkest period in the history of mankind.**

Notes:

BREAK-TIME (Slides # 36 - 37)

(Slide # 38)

MYSTERY BABYLON –
A PROSTITUTE "SEATED ON MANY WATERS"

Now let's consider where her primary location exists today:

> Then one of the seven angels who had the seven bowls came and said to me, "Come, I will show you the judgment of the **great prostitute who is seated on many waters,** ***Revelation 17:1***

Then the angel goes on to say:

> And the angel said to me, **"The waters** that you saw, where the prostitute is seated**, are peoples and multitudes and nations and languages.** ***Revelation 17:15***

The United States of America is also a nation seated on many waters both physically and symbolically.

- Physically, she is bordered east, west, and south by the two greatest oceans and by five great lakes in the north as well as mighty rivers in her interior.
- She also governs multitudes of peoples that come from many different nations and languages.
- She is the pride of the whole earth as well as being the focus of great jealousy from nations who envy her riches.

Notes:

____

____

____

____

____

____

____

(Slide # 39)

AMERICA – IN THE WORLD'S SPOTLIGHT

Key Points:

- America is not specifically mentioned in the bible, but why would it be? The bible was completed 2,000 years ago and no discovery of the western world would take place for another 1,000 years.

- However, the bible continually mentions countries from afar but describes them as countries in the north, south, east, and west.

Now, what country has made the greatest impact upon the growth of Christianity worldwide?
It is America that has been the greatest nation that has represented Christianity worldwide since the last page of the bible was written.

When Jesus teaches on events that precede His second coming, He warns of false teachers who will lead many astray, many in the church will betray others, etc.

>>>>>*And then many will fall away and betray one another and hate one another. And many false prophets will arise and lead many astray.* ***Matthew 24:10-11***

- Think about it! What other country has such a large Christian population that will fall away and betray many of His people?

And if we are presently on the verge of the Day of the Lord, as many of us believe, -- then the United States is the only nation that possesses both the commercial and religious characteristics of Mystery Babylon to the level reflected in the Book of Revelation.

When Jesus teaches on events that precede His second coming, He warns of false teachers who will lead many astray, many in the church will betray others, etc.

>>>>>*And then many will fall away and betray one another and hate one another. And many false prophets will arise and lead many astray.* ***Matthew 24:10-11***

- Think about it! What other country has such a large Christian population that will fall away and betray many of His people?

And if we are presently on the verge of the Day of the Lord, as many of us believe, -- then the United States is the only nation that possesses both the commercial and religious characteristics of Mystery Babylon to the level reflected in the Book of Revelation.

- Our nation may or may not be final location of Mystery Babylon, but in this current generation, the spirit of the whore is most prominent in the great cities of America.

Notes:

______

______

______

______

______

______

(Slide # 40)

AMERICA & ISRAEL – BOTH NATIONS FOUNDED UNDER GOD

America and Israel are the only nations ever founded from the beginning upon the purposes of Almighty God.

Israel was God's nation under the Old Covenant. The western world which was relatively unknown in biblical times represents the world of Christianity under the New Covenant.

America has been the most influential nation in the promotion of Christianity throughout the world. The Lord has obviously called America as a representative of the New Covenant and over the last four centuries, she has greatly influenced all the nations of the world with the gospel of Jesus Christ.

Godly leaders built this country under the biblical principles of justice, truth, and religious freedom.

These founding fathers were Europeans seeking freedom from persecution within the countries of Western Europe. They were the early pilgrims who pursued and honored the Lord.
Our present-day heritage of freedom, peace, and prosperity is the fruit of our forefather's obedience to and love for, the Lord Jesus Christ and His heavenly Father.

Notes:

______

______

______

______

(Slide # 41)

AMERICA – A NATION GONE TERRIBLY ASTRAY

Today, like ancient Israel, the United States of America is a nation gone terribly astray.

Key Points:

Like Babylon which was represented by the golden head in Nebuchadnezzar's dream, America certainly appears to be the home of the harlot woman who is the guiding source of the beast in this era.

A country that was founded on Christian principles has now chosen to throw off our Christian heritage and embrace the principles of Sodom and Gomorrah.

Today, in America, the voice of demons sounds quite pleasant. They are heard on television, in the newspapers, in theatres, in our classrooms, and even in many of our churches.

- They are voices that continually speak to us about living a happy and successful life but in reality, they conceal the truth that leads to true eternal happiness.
- Materialism, entertainment, pleasure-seeking, celebrity worship, abnormal sexual relationships, obsession with shopping and eating; these are our idols.
- We worship the sinful lifestyle that provides physical and emotional pleasure and we worship all those Hollywood type celebrities who continually encourage us in our idolatrous living.

Notes:

AMERICA – A NATION GONE TERRIBLY ASTRAY

Today, like ancient Israel, the United States of America is a nation gone terribly astray.

We have seen a tremendous decaying society rise up and control a former Christian nation. For example, today we are a nation where:

- **They have removed all prayer and bible study from our schools and in most governmental facilities – in cities and states throughout our country.**
- **A corrupt news media has brainwashed many of today's Americans into following the harlot who rides the beast.**
- **Abortion clinics have butchered tens of millions of babies over the last 40 years and today it appears that some states are now making it lawful to murder babies even after they are born. They also sell the body parts of these innocent young babies.**
- **We are now a country where our judicial system allows criminals more rights than their victims. Criminals using the motto "Black Lives Matter" (BLM) are murdering, raping, stealing, burning properties – yet they are considered "innocent" in our demonic city and state governments. Victims of these evil crimes are of no consequence to them.**
- **For they are secretly whoring with the Woman who rides the Beast, who is intent on doing away with police forces in order to allow these crimes that are extremely pleasing to their great whore – to continue.**
- **Where violent youth gangs and desperate drug addicts make many city streets unsafe – yet, they are continually supported by our increasingly leftist governments. Many of these addicts compromise these rioting mobs in our city streets – who desire to abolish our American heritage.**
- **Where violent and demonic TV, movies, video games, and drugs have spawned a dangerous belief system among the millennial generation of the 21st century.**
- **We are now a country that embraces a "godless lifestyle" that welcomes adultery, abortion, pornography, homosexuality, and same-sex marriages as a normal way of life.**

Notes:

(Slides # 44 - 46)

AMERICA – A NATION GONE TERRIBLY ASTRAY

Woe to those who call evil good and good evil, who put darkness for light and light for darkness, who put bitter for sweet and sweet for bitter! Woe to those who are wise in their own eyes, and shrewd in their own sight! ***Isaiah 5:20-21***

Sin is running rampant in our city streets; yet the great majority of American churches are strangely silent – they have lost their influence concerning the direction of our nation.

Key Points:

The testimony of the gospel message of Jesus Christ - being the one and only way to enter into the eternal kingdom - has become more and more silent - during this age where the internet and cell phones control the minds of so many Americans.

Demonically led leftists governments & peoples:

A wise man's heart inclines him to the right, but a fool's heart to the left. ***(Eccl.10:2)***

Sin and lawlessness have replaced righteousness and justice in our once great and mighty land.

Key Points:

- Power and riches have led a former nation of God into a great apostasy.
- The great prosperity experienced in this nation has lulled many of God's people into following cross-less, painless gospel.
- Sadly, our nation no longer worships the Lord who blessed us with prosperity and established our religious freedoms.

Those who embrace these self-seeking lifestyles are among the worshippers of Mrs. Mystery Babylon, that adulterous whore who pretends to be the Bride of Christ.

Now - Are we entering into the "last days?"

Well, listen to the following verse in 2nd Timothy which describes the world's social system in the last days.

Godlessness in the Last Days

But understand this, that in the last days there will come times of difficulty. For people will be lovers of self, lovers of money, proud, arrogant, abusive, disobedient to their parents, ungrateful, unholy, heartless, unappeasable, slanderous, without self-control, brutal, not loving good, treacherous, reckless, swollen with conceit, lovers of pleasure rather than lovers of God, having the appearance of godliness, but denying its power. Avoid such people. **2 Timothy 3:1-5**

- Now, doesn't this sound like the common lifestyle of today's America?

A country that was founded on Christian principles has now chosen to throw off our Christian heritage and embrace the principles of Sodom and Gomorrah. These cities were also burned up in a single day.

(Slides # 47 - 48)

AMERICA – A NATION GONE TERRIBLY ASTRAY

Sadly, our nation no longer worships the Lord who blessed us with prosperity and established our religious freedoms.

Key Points:

A country that was founded on Christian principles has now chosen to throw off our Christian heritage and embrace the principles of Sodom and Gomorrah. These cities were also burned up in a single day.

- Righteousness and justice in our once great and mighty land has been replaced by sin and lawlessness.
- America has fallen into the same trap as ancient Israel; power and riches has led a former nation of God into a great apostasy.

Jesus Himself tells us that a nation divided against itself cannot stand. And today, we are no longer the United States of America – we are now the Divided States of America (DSA).

Key Points:

Is modern America, among those great historical empires, represented by Mystery Babylon who rides and steers the beast? Probably!

- **At any rate, there can be no doubt that our country loves to fornicate with the lady who rides the beast.**

And we must be aware that if the rise of the Antichrist is coming within our generation, - then obviously America will be the last of the nations represented by this harlot woman.
If so, she will soon burn in a single day.

Today, the United States is the only nation with the characteristics of Mystery Babylon - to the level reflected in the Book of Revelation.

In this generation, - the spirit of the whore is most prominent in the great cities of America.

I personally believe that our once great and mighty nation - is shortly heading - for a great and terrible fall.

(Slide # 49)

This will be a time of tremendous destruction and grief among Americans; yet this period of intense hardships will open many hearts to the gospel message proclaimed by the anointed messengers of God.

For these are the ones that will hear the calling from our Lord in Isaiah 60:1-2

> Arise, shine, for your light has come, and the glory of the Lord has risen upon you. For behold, darkness shall cover the earth, and thick darkness the peoples; but the Lord will arise upon you, and his glory will be seen upon you. ***Isaiah 60:1-2***

Notes:

BREAK-TIME **(Slides # 50 - 51)**

(Slides # 52 - 54)

THE BABYLONIAN WHORE & FALSE CHRISTIANITY

Key Points:

A woman in Scripture is frequently symbolic of the God's chosen people.

- **In the Old Testament, Israel is the Wife of Yahweh, while in the New Testament; the church is the Bride of Christ.**

The Old Testament frequently identifies the nation of Israel as the Wife of the Lord.

- She was immensely blessed by her Husband, but later went whoring after other gods.
- She also sacrificed her children to these gods much like today's abortionists.[74]

Thus, it is apparent in Scripture that a spiritual harlot is one who claims to be faithful to her Husband; yet runs after the gods of other religions.

- This spiritual harlot in America - will help blend Christianity with other faiths - and continue to dilute the true gospel message of Jesus Christ.

The counterfeit churches in America also claim to be the true church. And outwardly, she may look like the church, but she is really the harlot woman who embraces the worldly lifestyle.

Key Points:

She fornicates with those who dwell on the earth and invents a Christianity of her own - which may not deny Jesus as a good man sent by God, but will trample on the need for His redemptive blood - and encourage her followers to joyfully embrace the worldly lifestyle.

- Her churches are filled with false teachings that are designed to support her adulterous lifestyle and provide assurance that she is loved of God.

For example - the preaching of "tolerance" is a misleading doctrine promoted by the enemy to effectively weaken the truth of the biblical gospel.

- The "tolerance" doctrines assume that man is not sinful, but basically good, even if at various times in life, they may need counseling help.

- Eventually, if Christians proclaim that Jesus Christ is the one and only way to eternal life, the time is coming when they will be maligned as bigots, fanatics, judgmental, unloving and therefore, a hindrance in the establishment of a peaceful society.
- This religious prostitute will side with those governmental authorities who insist that the church must be "tolerant" of those who believe that there are many ways to eternal life.
- She will help blend Christianity with other faiths and continue to dilute the true gospel of Jesus Christ.

This is currently the vision of the leaders of the emergent church movement as well as all those dominations who teach that all who believe in their worldly gods will also experience eternal life with Christians.

[74] Ezekiel 16:8-22

(Slide # 55)

AMERICA – BIBLICAL DOCTRINES REPLACED BY IDOLATRY

Today in America, numerous congregations avoid the preaching of the cross and the discipline of the Lord.

Paul was certainly speaking to these popular American churches - who are led by false teachings:

For the time is coming when people will not endure sound teaching, but having itching ears they will accumulate for themselves teachers to suit their own passions, and will turn away from listening to the truth and wander off into myths. *2 Timothy 4:3-5*

Key Points:

Many of these churches are filled to overflowing to hear their pillow prophets teach a gospel of prosperity and easy believism; while the few voices declaring the impending judgment of God are virtually ignored by many.

- These churches have a "Christian welfare mentality" that caters to the hurting spirit; giving out large doses of feel good teachings that empowers the ego of the listeners.
- They understand that it is much easier to speak the words that people want to hear which will allow them to grow in popularity - among those who want to continue in their worldly lifestyles.
- Christians are misled to jump into the resurrected life by a shortcut - that bypasses the continuing work of the cross in the believer's life.

The blindness existing within these churches is horrendous. **While individual churches continue to compete with one another for more people and more money, they remain virtually silent concerning the sin that is rapidly overtaking our nation.**

- Today, in most American churches, the leaders who claim to know His word fail to recognize the hour of judgment being at hand.

Instead of teaching people how to "think and grow rich," these churches should be encouraging one another to pursue the Lord and His holiness.

- **But - With their teaching and preaching of materialism, these churches are doing a better job of paving the way for the rise of the Antichrist - than preparing for the return of Jesus Christ.**

(Slides # 56 - 57)

MY PEOPLE – COME OUT OF BABYLON!

The call to come out of Babylon is first heard in the prophecy of Isaiah and is heard seven times in all, the last being in this chapter of Revelation.[75]

> Come out of her, my people, lest you take part in her sins, lest you share in her plagues; for her sins are heaped high as heaven, and God has remembered her iniquities. **Revelation 18:4-5**

Then He goes on to say in Rev 18:8

> For this reason, her plagues will come in a single day, death and mourning and famine, and she will be burned up with fire; for mighty is the Lord God who has judged her. **Rev. 18:8**

This call to come out of her does not mean that we are to physically leave our homes; unless of course, He calls us to physically relocate.

- It is a call to depart from the idolatrous pleasures of the world and turn to serving in the army of our Lord Jesus Christ throughout our lifetime where we will continually fight against the spiritual forces of darkness – that keep so many of our family and friends in bondage.

Notes:

____

____

____

(Slides # 58 - 59)

WHO ARE THE CHRISTIANS WHO ARE IN MYSTERY BABYLON?

If you are in a church that does not proclaim the following foundational truths; <u>COME OUT NOW</u>!

- Jesus Christ is God's Son who came to earth to pay the penalty of death for all those who believe on His Name.
- Jesus Christ is truly divine and existed from all eternity as the Son of God. He is the Word of God that was present when creation was spoken into being.
- Jesus Christ paid the death penalty for the sins of all those who repent and embrace Him as their Savior.
- It was by His sacrifice on the Cross that the sins of all who believe in Him have been washed away for all of the guilt of those who believe in Jesus has been nailed to the Cross and they have been set free forever by His glorious sacrifice.
- Jesus Christ is the one and only way to eternal salvation. There is no other way.

[75] Isaiah 48:20; 52:11; Jeremiah 50:8-9; 51:6-8; Zechariah 2:6-7; 2 Corinthians 6:17-18; Revelation 18:4-8

Notes:

____

____

____

____

____

____

(Slides # 60 - 61)

COME OUT NOW!

False teachers occupying many of the pulpits in our churches may not admit to their unbelief in the above truths concerning our Lord and His Word.

They may remain silent in order to maintain their attendance numbers. However, if their message does not regularly embrace the above truths, it is a warning sign; come out now!

A CHURCH THAT:

- Compromises the truth that the Bible is not inerrant, but is simply a book written by men which contains some truths, but also contains false beliefs. **Come out now!**
- Teaches that "tolerance" is the ultimate expression of true love for others. That man is basically good and that we must be tolerant of those who profess different beliefs in God. **Come out now!**
- Teaches that the God of Abraham, Isaac, and Jacob is the same Allah that the Muslims worship. That the gods of Buddhism and Hinduism are the same as the God of Christianity. They just have different names depending on one's culture. **Come out now!**
- Teaches that financial prosperity is available to each of us if we will only begin to tithe our limited resources to their individual ministries. That our personal pleasure and financial security is how one measures success in this life. **Come out now!**
- If you are in a church that is more focused on your blessings than with our Lord who gave those blessings; where financial prosperity has prioritized your life; where your comforts have replaced the Cross in your life; where entertainment has replaced evangelism in the workplace. **Come out now!**
- If you are in a church that ridicules Christians who will not deny their faith that Jesus is the only path to eternal life, you are in Mystery Babylon. **Come out now!**

These are some of the idolatrous doctrines of Mystery Babylon and the true people of God must run from these lies that are intended to compromise our faith in God and bring about a great smile on the face of Satan.

- Additionally, if you are in a denominational church that teaches that membership in their church is the only way to eternal life – you are in Mystery Babylon – Come Out Now!

Now who are those that come out of the world?

Scriptures tell us in 1st John 5:4-5

For everyone who has been born of God overcomes the world. And this is the victory that has overcome the world— our faith. Who is it that overcomes the world except the one who believes that Jesus is the Son of God?

Notes:

____

____

____

____

____

____

____

____

____

____

(Slides # 62 - 63)

"ABOUT FACE"

Those with military experience are very familiar with the command "about-face" which is a command to immediately turn sharply 180 degrees from the direction you are currently facing.

- It is also a command used by our Commander-in-Chief **who calls us to "turn" from our sins**; then He will remove the veil which is blinding us from the truth and put us on the path of growing in spiritual maturity.

- This willingness to turn in an **"about-face" will suddenly cause us to see ourselves as we truly are and thus, our need for a Savior**.

- **All of God's champions will occasionally go astray** and veer from the course that the Lord directs. However, like Moses, David, or Paul, **they all have one thing in common**; when confronted with their blindness, they will readily turn in an "about-face" and return to following their Commander.

What will Christians do when our Commander-in-Chief commands us to "about-face"?

- Will they obey Him or listen to other subordinate commanders, such as some church leaders who tell us that the Commander-in-Chief really meant **"right-face"** since it is much easier to follow that path.

- **But a partial turn will eventually lead us away from the path that Jesus is going** and even though other leaders tell us that we are moving rightly, we are straying further and further from His direction.

- Some other false commanders may convince us that the command was really **"at-ease";** just keep coming and giving to the church and God will be pleased.

- Eventually the time comes when the Commander-in-Chief gives the command **"forward march"**; only those who heard and obeyed the command **"about-face"** will be equipped to follow the King of kings and the Lord of lords in the direction He is heading.[76]

"Christian warriors, we are called to fight the forces of darkness, and not run from this battle - that is keeping so many of our family and friends in bondage to Mystery Babylon, the Woman who rides the Beast!"

(Slides # 64 - 65)

COME OUT OF BABYLON - NOW!

For there is a day coming when Christians will need to make a definite decision as to who they will serve. Just as the prophet Elijah spoke to the Israeli peoples on Mount Carmel:

"How long will you go limping between two different opinions? If the Lord is God, follow him; but if Baal, then follow him." ***1 Kings 18:21***

Key Points:

The present day application of this demand might be:

- If the Christ of Scripture be the true Savior, then surrender to Him. But if the false Christ being commonly preached in many pulpits is your savior, then go ahead and follow him.

- One who demands the denying of self and another who allows the gratifying of self cannot both be right.

- One who insists on separation from the world and another who permits you to enjoy its friendship cannot both be right.

- One who came to bring division among the people and another who came to unite the world cannot both be right.

God will not accept a divided heart; He will have all or none. He will permit no compromise.

WAKE UP & COME OUT NOW!

[76] Al Houghton, *Word at Work* (Newsletter Volume XXI, Number IX, Chapter 10)

Notes:

(Slide # 66)

THE NEXT SESSION:

First Read: Revelation 14 & 15 plus 16:1-9

THE LAST HARVEST FOLLOWED BY DESTRUCTION

- Dark Stories are always Followed by Light.
- "Blessings & Warnings" in Seven Major Events.
- One: The Lamb & 144,000 on Mt Zion.
- Two: The Angel & the Everlasting Gospel.
- Three: The Fall of Babylon.
- Four: Warning Against "Worshipping the Beast."
- Five: Blessed are Those who Die in the Lord from Now On.
- Six: The Harvest of the Earth.
- Seven: God's Wrath Falling Upon the World of Evil.
- Heaven Celebrates while the World Blasphemies.
- The Final Judgments of our Lord Begin.
- Pouring Out the Bowls of God's Wrath

THE LAMB OF GOD - OUR TRUE "COMMANDER-IN-CHIEF"

The days are rapidly approaching when a tremendous separation will take place among mankind.

Yet, during this present era of warfare, He reigns as our Commander-in-Chief and His Name continues to be the battle cry for those warriors who fight daily for righteousness and truth.

His name is Jesus, Our Lord, Our King, Our Commander-in-Chief

- **A truly mighty Leader who would never delegate assignments to His people that He Himself wouldn't readily embrace.**
- **A Commander that Christian warriors will readily follow not matter the danger or what costs have to be paid.**
- **These are warriors whose deepest desire is to hear Jesus welcome them with the following words when they enter into His presence:**

> **......... 'Well done, good and faithful servant. You have been faithful over a little; I will set you over much. Enter into the joy of your master.' *Matthew 25:21***

MINISTRY and RESOURCES

To arrange for speaking engagements with Dr. Don Bell use the following contact information:

Email: Dr.Don.Bell@mcgmin.com
Review Dr. Bell's profile at: www.mcgmin.com/authors.html
Call: (888) 575-9626

This workbook, Keep What is Written, follows Dr. Bell's lesson series available on www.equippingwatchmen.com. This important lesson series is based on the following book:

God's Anointed Warriors
By Dr. Donald Bell (available now.)

This book brings 21st century clarity to prophetic events recorded in the book of Revelation and the Lord's calling for warrior-spirited Christians of this generation.

We are right on the verge of devastating events that will create great fear and chaos throughout the world and especially in our increasingly immoral and comfort-seeking nation.

The reader is encouraged to follow Dr. Donald Bell in his in-depth study of Scripture that will bring greater clarity to numerous end-time events recorded in the Book of Revelation -events which are currently unfolding before our very eyes.

ISBN 978-1-943412-08-2

Published by -
Wilderness Voice Publishing
Canon City, Colorado USA
www.wvpbooks.com

This valuable resource can be obtained by the following:

- Amazon.com - Search: God's Anointed Warriors By Dr. Donald Bell
- Order from your local bookstore: ISBN 978-1-943412-08-2
- Wilderness Voice Publishing: https://www.mcgmin.com

www.ingramcontent.com/pod-product-compliance
Lightning Source LLC
LaVergne TN
LVHW080922110826
845155LV00039B/178

* 9 7 8 1 9 4 3 4 1 2 0 6 8 *